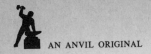

AN ANVIL ORIGINAL

THE MUCKRAKE YEARS

D1563382

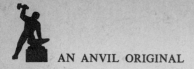

AN ANVIL ORIGINAL

THE MUCKRAKE YEARS

DAVID MARK CHALMERS
University of Florida

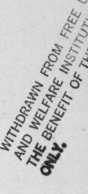

D. VAN NOSTRAND COMPANY

New York   Cincinnati   Toronto   London   Melbourne

Cover illustration by E. W. Kemble, originally in *Collier's, The National Weekly* (June 23, 1906), 37:5

D. Van Nostrand Company Regional Offices:
New York   Cincinnati   Millbrae

D. Van Nostrand Company International Offices:
London   Toronto   Melbourne

Library of Congress Catalog Card Number 73–14370
ISBN: 0–442–20116–8

Published by D. Van Nostrand Company
450 West 33rd Street, New York, N. Y. 10001

Published simultaneously in Canada by
Van Nostrand Reinhold Ltd.

10 9 8 7 6 5 4 3 2 1

For VERA and MICHAEL KRAUS

Preface

In 1909, a young Land Office investigator was fired by President William Howard Taft for questioning the legality of an Alaskan coal lands give-away to a Morgan-Guggenheim syndicate. Almost sixty years later, in 1967, a Defense Department investigator was fired for revealing billion dollar cost over-runs by prime aircraft contractors. The newly merged, once proud Pennsylvania and New York Central Railroads were wrecked by insider manipulations, and the national government often looked the other way where the meat and drug industries and mine safety were concerned. Revelation of Wall Street pursuit of insurance company assets in 1905 had brought an investigation and regulation of the industry. In the 1960s and 1970s, it was the conglomerate, rather than the banking house, that reached out for insurance company assets. Although there was no special "House of Mirth" in Washington, D.C. to handle payoffs, appreciative large-scale campaign contributions knew no party lines.

Muckraking was still considered distasteful and fascinating. General magazines such as *The Saturday Evening Post, Look,* and *Life* sought to stem their decline with classic muckrake fact stories. The major networks and newspapers set up what they more politely called investigatory teams, but they made no bones about calling columnist Jack Anderson a "muckraker"—and he won a Pulitzer Prize for it in 1972.

During the muckrake years at the beginning of the twentieth century, the United States took the major steps toward making its economy a regulatory capitalist system. More than half a century later, the problems of how to restrain private economic power and direct it toward the public good were still unsolved. The muckrake years were not over.

This manuscript exists through the encouragement of Louis L. Snyder, and the help of Michael Gordon and Jean Chalmers.

David M. Chalmers

Contents

Part I

THE MUCKRAKERS

CHAPTER 1

Turn of the Century America

Theodore Roosevelt wrote in his *Autobiography* in 1913 that "When I became President, the question as to the *method* by which the United States Government was to control the corporations was not yet important. The absolutely vital question was whether the Government had power to control them at all. This question had not yet been decided in favor of the United States Government." The struggle for control of the corporations and concentrated wealth was the issue that gave the Progressive Era its name. From it emerged the beginnings of the American regulatory capitalist system and of the modern American presidency.

In 1900 the American economy was increasingly dominated by giant corporations, and neither Congress nor the President had what could be called an economic program other than balancing the budget, keeping the tariff high, and paying obligations in gold. Congress was the policy-making arm, such as it was, and the President's duty was to carry out the laws it made. By 1912 the government was using the Sherman Antitrust Law to attack the trusts, and the Interstate Commerce Commission had been strengthened and was to become the model for other regulatory commissions. Laws had been passed for the inspection of meat and to protect the quality of food and drugs. Conservation was a national issue. The country was on the way to the popular election of senators, women's suffrage, the Federal Reserve System, and the income tax. The NAACP had been founded, the restriction of child and female labor and of workingmen's hours was being agitated, and the government was soon to offer rural credits to the farmers and highway money to the states.

The President had become the domestic policy maker and he guided his programs through the Congress. In the election of 1912, there were four major candidates. Only William Howard Taft was considered a conservative, while the reform Governor of New Jersey, Woodrow Wilson, won over the Progressive Party candidate Theodore Roosevelt and the Socialist Eugene Victor Debs. Together the three reformers gathered 77 percent of the vote.

Reform ferment had already been agitating many cities and states, but during the early years of the twentieth century it became a national concern and movement. Between 1903 and 1912, a group of journalists, whom President Roosevelt caustically labeled "muckrakers," filled the new popular magazines with detailed "fact-stories" about big business corruption and social problems. They helped make the middle classes concerned about politics and social conditions. In doing so, they played a crucial role in deciding the question of control of the corporations—of which Roosevelt wrote—in favor of the national government.

The United States in the Twentieth Century. When the assassin's bullet killed William McKinley and made Theodore Roosevelt president in 1901, the United States was becoming an urban and industrial nation and a world power. When the Constitution had been written less than 120 years before, the thirteen former colonies, all hugging the Atlantic coast, had a population of no more than 4,000,000 people. Twenty percent of these were slaves. In 1901 the nation stretched 3,000 miles to the Pacific Ocean and 1,500 miles from the Canadian border to the Rio Grande. There were forty-five states (Oklahoma would gain statehood in 1907, and Arizona and New Mexico in 1912) with a population of 76,000,000.

Agricultural America. When Thomas Jefferson doubled the land size of the United States by the purchase of the Louisiana Territory in 1803, he believed that he had made America an agricultural nation for 100 generations to come. The land did not last 100 years. In a famous paper read to the American Historical Association, meeting at the Columbian Exposition in Chicago in 1893, the historian Frederick Jackson Turner noted that the frontier as a continuous line between settled and vacant land no longer existed. The American farmer was no longer a self-sufficient yeoman. He was producing a surplus for sale on an unpredictable world market. As agricultural output doubled after the Civil War, the prices of staples such as corn, wheat, and cotton fell. The farmer found that he had no control over the price he got for his grain and livestock. The millers and meat-packers to whom he sold and the banks, railroads, and manufacturers from whom he bought set the prices they paid and charged him. He was one of the last competitors in a world of growing economic concentration. Long hours, ceaseless toil, the uncertain struggle against nature, floods, droughts, and the grasshoppers, and the dullness and loneliness of life compared with that of the cities helped stir the farmers' protest movements of the 1870s, 1880s, and 1890s.

Mine, Mill, and City. In 1888 the shrewd steel maker Andrew Carnegie shifted his newest and most modern plant, the Homestead Works near Pittsburgh, from making rails to producing structures for America's growing cities. At the outbreak of the Civil War only one person in four was a townsman. By 1900, four in ten were. The number of cities with more than 50,000 people had risen from sixteen to seventy-eight. New York's population had tripled to 3,500,000 and Chicago was over 1,500,000. The cities were being fed by migrations from the farms and by immigration, primarily from southern and eastern Europe. Soon more than a million immigrants would enter the United States each year. Wages had risen slowly, though irregularly, and labor's real income advanced through the 1890s as agricultural prices fell. During the bitter depression years of the 1890s, real income dropped and strikes and unemployment were widespread. The weekly hours of work hovered close to sixty, and male mine and factory workers received less than ten dollars a week while women were paid about six dollars. Less than four percent of the labor force belonged to unions, and perhaps two-thirds of the workers lived close to poverty.

An Organizational Society. The keynote of twentieth-century America was organization. The railroads and modern communications had helped knit the "island communities" of America into an increasingly integrated nation. The year 1901 saw the formation of the American Socialist Party, the reorganization of the American Medical Association, and the first billion dollar corporation—J. P. Morgan's United States Steel Corporation.

During the years from about 1897 through 1901, an important change took place in the structure of American business. Promoted by the national money managers on Wall Street, firms merged or bought out each other to form huge concentrates which dominated much of American industry. Among the giants further centralization took place. Bankers, brokers, utilities, insurance companies, railroads, and industries were drawn together in great empires, largely dominated by the Rockefeller and Morgan interests. (*See Reading No. 1.*) In 1904, the respected financial authority John W. Moody, in his book *The Truth About The Trusts,* identified the Rockefeller group as including the National City and Hanover National Banks, the Equitable and Mutual Life Insurance Companies, the Gould railroads, most of the New York City utility franchise companies, the Widener-Elkins utility combine in Philadelphia, and many other large interests, in addition to a practical monopoly of the oil industry. Moody listed 440 industrial, franchise, and transportation trusts which together had a capitalization of more than $20,000,000,000. The 1900 census reported that 183 corporations controlled a fifth of the manufacturing output of the nation. The Industrial Commission reported to Congress two years later that most of the new giants were capitalized far beyond the cash value of their property, misrepresented to stock purchasers, and highly profitable to their promoters, and that they were likely to increase consumer prices and possibly decrease wages. The age of financial capitalism had arrived.

The Philosophy of *Laissez-faire*. The most important intellectual influence of the age was Charles Darwin's theory of evolution. Businessmen, conservatives, imperialists, and white supremacists used Herbert Spencer's version of evolution, which they called "the survival of the fittest," to justify business success, *laissez-faire,* and Anglo-Saxon dominance and empire. John D. Rockefeller, Jr. compared the Standard Oil Company with the American beauty rose, whose beauty could only be achieved by ruthlessly pruning all other buds. (*See Reading No. 1.*) To the directors of Standard Oil, this meant doing away with all competitors. The classical economics of Adam Smith, David Ricardo, and Thomas Malthus were combined with the lingering puritan doctrine that success and riches were the outward signs of morality. Together with the basic American goal of "making-a-million," they erected a wall against the idea of government intervention in the economy, except when it facilitated private economic development and profits.

The Philosophy of Reform. The problems of poverty and a clash of ideas led to a challenge of the American success ethic by some portions of the middle classes. Reformers, philosophers, scientists, and ministers maintained that *laissez-faire* was unchristian, unscientific, undemocratic, and unbearable. Reform Darwinists such as the sociologist Lester Frank Ward, the economist Richard T. Ely, and the philosopher William James argued for control of the environment and social planning. They maintained that science revealed the unfinished, plastic nature of man and his society, which could be improved through conscious human social effort. Young college graduates such as Jane Addams and Lillian Wald opened settlement houses and spearheaded reform in the urban ghettos. Realist and naturalist authors such as Stephen Crane, Frank Norris, and Theodore Dreiser wrote novels about poverty and life in the slums. Massachusetts Chief Justice Oliver Wendell Holmes, Jr. argued in *The Common Law* (1888) that law had to adjust to social conditions and needs. The highly successful corporation counsel Louis D. Brandeis opened up a new career as "the people's lawyer," by defending the efforts of the states to regulate labor conditions.

Misgovernment and Confusion. The leading English authority on America, Lord James Bryce, wrote in his *American Commonwealth* (1888) that the American cities were the worst governed units in the democratic world. Government in the United States was mainly local and state and inadequate to handle the exploding growth of the cities and the emergence of giant national corporations and interests. The national government was expected to do little, and presidents were selected by party bosses more concerned with holding on to power within their own states than with national policy. The prime nineteenth-century political issues were jobs (patronage), pensions, civil service, the tariff, and the currency.

Senators would have been indignant if the President of the United States had presented bills to be passed and then lobbied with the members and the general public for their adoption. Presidents Andrew Johnson, Ulysses S. Grant, Rutherford B. Hayes, James A. Garfield, Chester A. Arthur, Grover Cleveland, Benjamin Harrison, and William McKinley made no such attempts. They believed that law-making was up to the Congress and that the economy was to be directed by individual enterprise and regulated by competition. The Civil War had shown that the United States was one nation, indivisible, but that liberty and justice for all were the concern of the states. Occasional national regulatory efforts such as the income tax, the Sherman Antitrust Act and the Interstate Commerce Commission were either overturned by the courts or shorn of their powers. The states were not allowed much leeway for the regulation of industrial practices or labor conditions.

By the beginning of the twentieth century the organization and governance of American society had reached a state of great confusion. The confusion was nothing new, but by the 1900s, like everything else, it had reached a greater scale and was becoming popularly apparent. American individualism, economic competition, self-help, charity, local government, state responsibility, presidential passivity, and legislative dominance were not working. It was increasingly difficult to praise American democracy as a benevolent, wonder-working system.

Nineteenth-Century Reform Reports. The muckrake journalists were not the first who saw something wrong. Reformers had crusaded against the Tweed ring in New York City (1871) and the "spoils system" in the national government. Good government mayors such as William F. Havemeyer in New York (1872–1874), Grover Cleveland in Buffalo (1882–1883), and James D. Phelan in San Francisco (1897–1902) fought corruption. The great midwestern trio, Detroit's Hazen S. Pingree (1890–1897), Toledo's Samuel "Golden Rule" Jones (1897–1903), and Cleveland's Tom Johnson (1901–1909), attacked privilege and the problems of the poor as well. Some such as Grover Cleveland (New York) and Hazen Pingree (Michigan) had carried reform into the governor's mansion. Utopians, anarchists, Farmers' Alliancemen, and Knights of Labor had sought to escape from the market and industrial systems, while competitors and state governments had struggled against the Standard Oil Company.

The pessimistic aristocrat Henry Adams had written about Mammon in Washington and Jay Gould's ianipulations on Wall Street. Henry Demarest Lloyd's *Wealth Against Commonwealth* (1894) exposed Standard Oil's monopolistic drives. Henry George proposed a single tax on land as the way of handling "the association of poverty with progress" which was "the great enigma" of the times. Industry and labor fought actual wars in the mining camps of the West, in the railyards of the Midwest and East, and on the banks of the Monongahela River outside of Pittsburgh. The agrarian Populist Party condemned "the prolific womb of governmental injustice" which impoverished the farmers and bred "tramps and millionaires." Anti-monopoly was a popular enough cause to have produced the Sherman Anti-trust Act (1890) with few dissenting votes in Congress, although the law was soon to be emasculated by the Supreme Court.

Muckraking. It remained for a group of magazine journalists to pull together the threads of dissent and disenchantment and make the fullest report on the national confusion. In the years before World War I, the popular magazines were the national media (in the same way that radio and *Life* and *Time* magazines were to be in the 1930s, and television after World War II). It seemed as though everybody read them. In their articles the muckraking journalists gave the American people a popular course in sociology. Between 1903 and 1912, a small group of writers produced almost 2,000 detailed, factual articles on the national corruption and confusion. The accounts were complimented by editorials and cartoons, touted by flashy titles and glossy, beckoning covers which promised shocking revelations on the inside, and backed up by similarly sensational revelations and preachments in the local press. The style was accusatory. The subject matter was corruption. America was in crisis, somehow falling apart. Not only were the marketplace and its prime institution, the corporation, betraying America, but so were the local, state, and national governments and the American values of individualism and economic gain. The problems seemed to be everywhere.

CHAPTER 2

The Making of the Magazines

Technological Change. The popular magazines, like the great newspapers, were the product of a century-long revolution in the technology of putting print to paper. By 1900, printing was no longer done by a heavy metal plate which was hand-levered to press the paper down on a flat, stationary type bed (hence the name "printing press"). This method of printing had been in use since the fifteenth century when Johann Guttenberg developed the first-known wooden printing press. Three hundred years later, R. Hoe & Company of New York and London and its founder, Robert Hoe, had perfected a steam-driven press whose rollers forced the paper against rotating cylinders holding the type. Linotype ("line-O-type") machines replaced the hand setting of type. A similar machine, the "Monotype," produced the headlines, and a mold or "stereotype" of the print was created for the cylindrical plates. Paper was fed like an endless web from huge rolls into the machines. Powered by electricity, the presses printed on both sides of the paper and turned out more and more pages, faster and faster, at a lower per unit price.

Photoengraving, a process for reprinting illustrations, replaced woodcuts and hand engravings and reduced the cost by some ninety percent to less than twenty dollars a picture. A new process increased the range of shades between black and whites; R. Hoe & Co. built the presses to print multicolor illustrations as well as black and white. Pulpwood machines, developed first in Germany, reduced the price of paper, and the printing presses were equipped to cut and fold the pages to ready them for distribution.

The emergence of the popular magazines was not a product of technology alone. A handful of dynamic promoters and their imitators discovered the new middle-class market and combined technology with a price breakthrough, an advertising explosion, and a new kind of magazine journalism. The result was a critical forum from which the American middle classes took stock of a new urban, industrial, corporate America.

The Quality Magazines. Nineteenth-century America had its quality magazines and its pulps. The pulps came out irregularly and concentrated on fiction and scandal. The highbrow journals were mainly monthlies: *Harper's, Century, Scribner's*, and the *Atlantic Monthly*. By the end of the century the scholarly *North American Review* had begun to wheeze. Frank Luther Mott, the historian of the American magazines, described the quality journal as "leisurely in habit, literary in tone, retrospective, rather than timely, and friendly to the interests of the upper classes. It retained a certain aloofness, as a serene observer of the passing scene." It also sold for thirty-five cents.

A magazine reader in September of 1895 would have found the *Atlantic Monthly* prepared to inform him about the Civil War battle of Chickamauga, "The Plot of the Odyssey," "John Smith in Virginia," "President Polk's Administration," essays on "Samuel Taylor Coleridge" and a new "Standard Dictionary," plus fiction (usually serial), poetry, and comment on new books. *Harper's New Monthly Magazine*, forty-five years old in 1895, offered Part IX of "The German Struggle for Liberty" (against Napoleon), Part II of "Personal Recollections of Joan of Arc," "Notes on Indian Art," Owen Wister's "The Evolution of the Cow-puncher," Mark Twain on "Mental Telegraphy," and Richard Harding Davis' version of the adventures of "Three Gringos in Central America."

By 1900, an *Atlantic* critic noted, the journals were undergoing considerable change. The old-fashioned travel article had all but disappeared and there was a notable gain in short stories. Journalists turned their attentions to current affairs such as the "Spanish War" of 1898. At the same time that the newspapers' Sunday "supplements" were moving closer to magazine journalism, the journals were becoming more concerned with the problems of the day. Interest was increasingly focused on contemporary politics and business behavior, of which a recently emerged group of the journals were to become the most severe critics.

Advertising and the Popular Magazines. In the 1880s there were some 3,300 magazines in the United States. The serious ones of national reputation such as the *Atlantic* and *Century* cost 25 to 35¢ and reached circulation heights of as many as 100,000 copies. They did not demean themselves by carrying advertising. By 1905, the number of magazines had grown to over 6,000. A bright, highly political, socially-minded group of them cut their price to 10¢ and several were pushing close to monthly sales of half a million. In 1905 the popular *Ladies' Home Journal* sold close to a million copies. More than a hundred pages of advertising was not unusual. At the rate of $400 a page, advertising revenue might yield a journal more than $500,000 a year.

The widespread railroad and communication system, financial concentration in Wall Street, and great trusts such as the Standard Oil Company and the American Sugar Refining Company had created a national market in the United States. Each city no longer had its own slaughter house and flour mill. National products for national markets meant national advertising. James Buck Duke, owner of the American Tobacco Company, learned early the importance of putting the names of its Virginia Brights, Duke's Bests, Pets, and Sweet Caporals before the public. Monarch Bicycles, Quaker Oats, Eastman Kodak, Gilette Razors, Scott's Emulsion, Prudential Life Insurance, Hire's Root Beer, Uneeda Biscuits, and Lydia E. Pinkham's Vegetable Compound joined Pear's Soap and the book advertisements in the magazines, taking up more and more pages and bringing in high revenues.

Advertising success was not always a blessing for the magazines. A sudden rise in circulation through a popular series such as Ida Tarbell's "History of the Standard Oil Company" might double circulation. Since advertising rates had already been contracted, twice as many copies on the newsstands might well mean that the magazine was spending more to print the advertising than it was receiving for doing so. Although advertising rates eventually caught up with increased circulation, during the muckrake era there were numerous cases of magazines losing money on successful series. None, however, deliberately dropped subscribers and cut circulation to bring publishing costs down within the range of their advertisers' specialized need, as *The Saturday Evening Post* and *Look* were to do half a century later.

The large amounts of money which they handled tempted more than one successful publishing entrepreneur, such as S. S. McClure and Erman J. Ridgway, into disastrous speculative adventures. Furthermore, the dependence on such revenues made the magazines liable to pressure from advertisers on what to publish.

The Creators: John Brisben Walker, Frank Munsey, and S. S. McClure. While technology and an expanding market greatly influenced its growth, the cheap, popular magazine was essentially the product of three men: John Brisben Walker, Frank Munsey, and Samuel S. McClure. The owner and editor of *Cosmopolitan Magazine* from 1889–1905, John Brisben Walker was an imaginative hustler, whose careers included diplomacy, the army, iron manufacturing, real estate, newspaper reporting, and automobiles. He ran a lively illustrated magazine that constantly mixed schemes to buy Cuba from Spain, the founding of a correspondence course university, promotion of an international language, and investigations into the prospects of men flying, with good fiction and stories about the railroads, industry, war, and science.

Frank A. Munsey was a Horatio Alger hero come to life. A poor boy who began as a printer and telegrapher, he wanted to be a newspaper man, to associate with the wealthy, and to be someone. He struggled into the magazine business, making his way with boys' fiction in his *Argosy*. In 1891 he founded *Munsey's Magazine*, whose fiction he liked to brighten with pictures of exceptionally pretty girls—art studies, mind you, nothing salacious—which libraries sometimes found not quite acceptable. His competitor S. S. McClure once described Frank Munsey as the only editor better than himself: "If he likes a thing then everybody will like it." From the magazine business he moved into newspapers, buying, merging, or killing old standbys such as the New York *News*, the *Press*, the *Globe*, the *Sun*, and the *Telegraph*, and when he couldn't buy Ogden Reid's *Tribune*, he sold his *Herald* to it. At his death, the veteran editor William Allen White commented that Munsey had contributed to the journalism of his day "the talent of a meat packer, the morals of a money changer and the manners of an undertaker."

Samuel S. McClure's great love was magazine journalism. Immigrating from Ireland as a boy, he was desperately poor and eager for success. He was educated in the idealistic orthodoxy of the midwestern small town and Knox College in Galesburg, Illinois. This was a heady mixture of revivalism, Republicanism, and the legacies of John Brown, Abraham Lincoln, uplift, and success. McClure set up a fiction distribution syndicate, dashing back and forth across the Atlantic to sign up prominent English and American authors. Finally in 1893 he gathered together enough money to begin *McClure's Magazine* and immediately pushed it toward

success with the fiction of Robert Louis Stevenson, Rudyard
Kipling, and Anthony Hope, current topics of interest, and highly
popular series which tapped the current interest in Napoleon and
Abraham Lincoln.

Ten Cents a Copy. When *McClure's* first appeared in the
summer of 1893 it matched the literary quality of the expensive 25 to
35¢ magazines but was more highly illustrated and contemporary in
its articles. Its price was 15¢. John Brisben Walker, who had been
considering a lower price, cut *Cosmopolitan* to 12½¢, and the next
month *Munsey's* went down to 10¢ a copy, with a year's subscription
for a dollar. It took another two years for *McClure's* to take the final
plunge to 10¢. It was a bold and successful action for them all, and
Frank Munsey had been the bravest. The American Newspaper
Company was an almost monopolistic distributor. It controlled the
newsstands, and the share of the price it wanted left slim return for a
monthly that sold for only a dime. American News wanted to keep
5½ cents of each dime the customer paid. Munsey offered American
News 3 cents a copy and, with an advertising campaign underwrit-
ten by credit from Charles Dana's New York *Sun*, stimulated a
demand for his magazine and brought the distributor to his terms.

Munsey's victory over the newspaper distributors was a big
contribution to the as yet unborn muckrake crusade, and his only
one. Frank Munsey never became a muckraker. He admired the
successful men too much to ever scourge or condemn them. John
Brisben Walker was not the criticizing type either, and it was not
until William Randolph Hearst bought *Cosmopolitan* that it joined
the muckrake pack. However, the instrument had been created.
Harold Wilson in *McClure's Magazine and the Muckrakers* (1970)
described the new popular monthlies which Walker, Munsey, and
McClure had created as "low-priced, heavily illustrated, advertise-
ment-laden," with "contents emphasizing youthful optimism, self-
improvement, and success."

The Making of a Crusade. It remained for S. S. McClure to turn
the monthlies to the study of the underside of American society,
although there were others who claimed the credit of being first.
Accounts of corruption had not waited until the twentieth century—
and on occasion the muckrakers were liable to trace their profession
back to Jesus of Nazareth. William Rockhill Nelson's Kansas City
Star had its say about bribery, boodle, and the doings of the great
monopolies. So did Victor Lawson's Chicago *Daily News* and Joseph

Pulitzer's New York *World*. William Randolph Hearst's New York *Journal* was just as eager for the fight—and perhaps even the goals—as any of them. But it was Sam McClure who combined upper-class concern with popular taste for scandal and excitement and prepared it for middle-class taste. It was he who discovered muckraking and made a profession and a movement of it.

CHAPTER 3

The Discovery of the Muckrake

Nobody started out to rake "muck." When it all began, Thomas Lawson was busy manipulating the stocks of Amalgamated Copper. Upton Sinclair was on the way to socialism, pouring out his despairing naturalistic novels. C. P. Connolly had left Butte, Montana and was practicing law in New Jersey. The other future muckrakers were all newspapermen. Trained fact-gatherers, they were working their way east from western and midwestern journals to the major New York papers and eventually to the magazines.

Beginnings. Ida Tarbell had been brought into the magazine fold in 1892. S. S. McClure had burst into her small apartment in Paris with a hundred plans for his journal, signed her up, and borrowed forty dollars. It was Ida Tarbell who produced McClure's immensely successful series on Napoleon and on Abraham Lincoln. With the new century, concern over monopoly was growing, and S. S. McClure thought that his magazine should do a series on one of the trusts. An editorial conference decided on oil, and Ida Tarbell, who had grown up in the oil country of western Pennsylvania, started gathering material.

McClure had hurried Ray Stannard Baker to the war-torn Pennsylvania anthracite coal fields to look into the condition of the miners who were not supporting the strike. Baker had written approvingly about the efficiency of American industry and was enraptured with the romance of private industrial collectivism and the individualism of the non-union workers, but he dug deeply into the conditions in the fields. Meanwhile, Lincoln Steffens, one of an over-abundant supply of editors at *McClure's*, came up with an account of municipal corruption in St. Louis. The editorial office in New York became excited and sent him to dig up more in Minneapolis.

The January, 1903, *McClure's Magazine* contained its usual fare of romance and mystery fiction, plus reports from the worlds of medicine, English letters and manners, and an Abyssinian pilgrim in Jerusalem. It also offered Lincoln Steffens' lead article "The Shame of Minneapolis: The Rescue and Redemption of a City that Was Sold Out" (with a facsimile of the grafters' ledger), the third chapter of Ida Tarbell's "History of the Standard Oil Company," and an article by Ray Stannard Baker on "The Right to Work, The Story of the Non-striking Miners." On the final page was S. S. McClure's editorial "Concerning Three Articles in this Number of McClure's and a Coincidence that May Set Us Thinking." (*See Reading No. 2.*)

In the editorial, McClure pointed out that together the articles constituted "an arraignment of American character" which could be summed up as "The American Contempt of Law." "Capitalists, workingmen, politicians, citizens—all breaking the law, or letting it be broken." Who was left to uphold it? The lawyers, the judges, and the churches were just as lawless and corrupt. The colleges did not understand. All were taking care of themselves and leaving the public to pay for it. The final cost, McClure summed up, would be the liberty of the people. If his analysis of the causes was only weakly developed, S. S. McClure at least had zeroed in on a major national problem and missed nothing of the potential importance of the Steffens, Tarbell, and Baker articles. Muckraking had officially begun.

Lincoln Steffens. Joseph Lincoln Steffens' father was a wealthy Sacramento businessman and one of the early settlers of California. He sent his son to the University of California and after that to a series of European universities. When Lincoln Steffens arrived back in New York, with a wife and no job or profession, he found a letter from his father telling him that he was on his own. Luckily Steffens got a newspaper job and quickly worked his way up from crime reporter on the *Evening Post* to city editor of the *Commercial-Advertiser.* Steffens was a born "insider." His seeming personal detachment and his cool poise and quick wit somehow led men to trust him. He was to become a first rate interviewer, counting among his good friends crooks, policemen, bosses, reformers, businessmen, and Theodore Roosevelt.

The Shame of the Cities. Steffens' account of Circuit-Attorney (later Governor of Missouri) Joseph W. Folk's fight against corruption in St. Louis made good reading, and so *McClure's* sent him out for more. *The Shame of the Cities* became his most famous contribution to the muckrake era and his best known writing until he relived it all, and more, in *The Autobiography of Lincoln Steffens* in 1931. In St. Louis ("Tweed Days in St. Louis" and "The Shamelessness of St. Louis") Steffens showed the "best" citizens buying politicians, franchises, and special privileges. In "The Shame of Minneapolis" he exposed the mayor and the police as the leaders of vice and crime. As in St. Louis, the "good citizens" opposed attempts to punish the guilty, and the boodlers stayed in office through manipulation of political party loyalty. In "Pittsburg: A City Ashamed" he discovered both police and financial corruption. Boss Christopher Megee ruled by giving the Pennsylvania Railroad and the corporations what they wanted and by sparing an indifferent citizenry the burden of self-government. Steffens called "Philadelphia: Corrupt and Contented," the "worst-governed city in the country." A state machine controlled all levels of government, and the people settled for the "appearance" of order. Steffens found "Chicago: Half Free and Fighting On," with a skilled, reform-minded Municipal Voters' League playing the regular parties off against each other. In his New York article, subtitled "Good Government to the Test," he pushed hard for Seth Low's reform ticket in the hope of rousing civic pride to beat the Democratic Tammany machine. The need, he argued, was not just occasional revolts, but continuous good government. The problem was that the American people seemed opposed only to disorderly scandal, not graft and corruption.

In summing up his conclusions, Steffens said that his purpose had been "to sound for the civic pride of an apparently shameless citizenship." Later in his *Autobiography*, Steffens cultivated an air of scholarly detachment, but in 1903 he hoped for practical results and had particularly tried to help the reformers. He had found that the corruption was not caused by a single class or ethnic stock. Rather it was produced by a combination of the big businessmen, the politicians, the "good citizens," the commercial spirit, the political party system, and the "treason" of the political leaders. The big businessmen sought to loot rather than service their communities. The politicians organized the communities for sale. The "good citizens" were too neglectfully busy to demand proper government. The commercial spirit was motivated by profit and greed, instead of civic patriotism. The political party system created false and easily manipulated loyalties, and the political leaders sold out the people who elected them.

In his articles, Steffens tried to touch civic pride in order to create a steady demand for good government. Whenever he discovered it, he seemed to find that it took an exceptional man—strong, honest, untouched by the "pulls" of self-interest—to lead. Steffens' articles helped focus attention on the extent of urban corruption and pointed out that "business government" was the cause, not the solution to the problem. (*See Reading No. 3.*) Steffens did not discuss the problems of race, poverty, monopoly, labor, or the other social concerns of the times; he concentrated solely on business corruption and public apathy.

The Corruption of the States. Capitalizing on the success of his municipal exposés, Steffens next had a go at the states: "Folk's Fight for Missouri," "Chicago's Appeal to Illinois," "Wisconsin: Representative Government Restored," "Rhode Island: A Corrupted People," "Ohio: A Tale of Two Cities," and two articles on "New Jersey: A Traitor State." It was a logical development of his studies of the cities. As Steffens wrote in his opening article, the stream of political corruption tied together all levels of government and society. (*See Reading No. 4.*)

By 1904–05 Lincoln Steffens had polished his style of interviewing and writing. There was less rhetoric than in his city articles and the stories were better told. Everyone talked with him, and many confided. There seemed to be prestige in being interviewed by the renowned journalist. After he had investigated the machine in Cincinnati, Boss Cox asked him, "What do you think of it?"

"Pretty good," I said.

"Pretty——!" He was too disgusted to finish. "Best you ever saw," he retorted, firmly.

"Well, I can't tell," I said. "My criterion for a graft organization is, How few divide the graft? How many divide it here?"

"Ain't no graft," he grumbled.

"Then it's a mighty poor thing."

He pondered a moment. Then, "How many do you say divides up here?"

"Three at least," I said. "You and Garry Herman and Rud Hynicka."

"Ugh!" he grunted, scornfully, and wagging one finger slowly before my face, he said: "There's only one divides up here."

Leadership. Steffens was particularly adept at drawing action pictures of the men who governed America. Most of the journalists of exposure similarly personified their message. It was a technique they learned from fiction, particularly the short story—the reigning feature of the popular magazines. Their message was seldom that reform would be accomplished by the replacement of evil men and bad government by good men and good government, even though it seemed this way to later historians and perhaps to much of their magazine audience. The ability to draw the world in human pictures gave the magazines much of their success, and Steffens was the master at it. His stories centered on the dominant men such as Rhode Island's Senator Nelson W. Aldrich, "the arch-representative of protected privileged business," and Mayor Tom Johnson who had the "dangerous ambition" to make Cleveland an honest, well-run city with representative government.

Steffens hammered a simple message at his readers. Special privilege was at the root of American corruption. The leadership of outstanding men was necessary to awaken the American people to alert, aware citizenship. These were also the themes of his "Upbuilder" articles for *American Magazine* on the New Jersey reformers Mark Fagan and Everett Colby, San Francisco's Rudolph Spreckles, W. S. U'Ren in Oregon, and Denver's "Kids' Judge" Ben Lindsey. Lincoln Steffens had started out calling this sense of popular responsibility "self government" or "representative government." By 1908, he was referring to it as "practical Christianity."

Practical Christianity. In his articles, Steffens told his stories of the corruptors and the upbuilders. He exhorted society's-leaders to lead, and the citizens to act as citizens. In a 1910–1911 series on industrial corruption for *Everybody's*, he poked about uncomfortably into Wall Street and the organization of the national economy, but his grasp was weak. It was on the subjects of leadership and citizenship that he felt most at home, but his role was to call for it rather than produce it.

Twice he tried to take a direct hand. Two leaders of the Structural Iron Workers Union, J. B. and J. J. McNamara, were charged with the dynamiting of the anti-labor Los Angeles *Times* in which twenty-one people died. Labor was sure that the two men were innocent, and Socialist Job Harriman stood a good chance of being elected mayor of Los Angeles. Organized business was sure the McNamara brothers were guilty, and the evidence began to indicate the same thing. The McNamaras' lawyer was Clarence Darrow, who wanted to try and save their lives by pleading them guilty. Lincoln Steffens sought to work out the details of a compromise whereby a lenient punishment might cool off the mounting labor-capital bitterness. He conducted negotiations between all parties and thought he had a promise of industrial cooperation in Los Angeles. However, the sentences were harsh and none of the agreements held up. In Boston, Steffens tried his practical Christianity again. His plan was to bring the bosses and the businessmen together into a civic reform combination. This didn't work either. Society seemed to listen carefully to Lincoln Steffens' diagnoses of social ills, but it did not pay much attention to his prescriptions.

Ida Tarbell. Others were to write more spectacularly, but Ida Tarbell gave class to the new movement of exposure. "The History of the Standard Oil Company" was the most impressive piece of work muckraking produced. Ida Tarbell was a dignified and determined woman. Influenced by the conversations of her mother's feminist friends, she rejected the "trap of marriage"—to her later regret—to seek a career as a writer. Her biographies of Napoleon and Abraham Lincoln made a big contribution to *McClure's* success. When the decision was made to study one of the great trusts, Standard Oil was picked, and Ida Tarbell was a logical choice to undertake the long, hard research involved.

The History of the Standard Oil Company. She began work in the fall of 1901, and the *History* ran in eighteen installments from November of 1902 through the spring of 1904. Miss Tarbell (her co-workers, respectfully, never called her Ida) had grown up in the oil region of western Pennsylvania and had been much moved by Henry Demarest Lloyd's pioneering attack on Standard Oil in *Wealth Against Commonwealth* (1894). She plowed through court records and Congressional and commission reports and interviewed men who had fought Standard Oil in the fields. Standard Oil Vice-President Henry H. Rogers got in touch with her through Mark Twain. For a while Ida Tarbell went regularly to Standard's headquarters at 26 Broadway in New York to discuss her material with Rogers, but when her article on Standard's espionage methods was published, the company cut off all contact.

In November of 1902, her first article described the birth of the oil industry in northwestern Pennsylvania. The dark-green, evil-smelling, scummy "rockoil" which salt producers had skimmed off the top of their wells was discovered to have commercial possibilities. At first it was sold as patent medicine; Seneca Oil was the most famous brand. Then local mill owners became interested in it as a lubricator and luminant. Finally in 1859, in Titusville, the first real well was brought in. Men and money rushed to the region to put down wells along every rocky run and creek. Wagons, flatboats, railroads, and pipelines joined to get crude oil to the refineries. Despite wildly fluctuating markets, speculation, and discrimination by the Erie, New York Central, and Pennsylvania Railroads, the oil men built their brawling shanty towns among the derricks on the muddy flats of the oil country. Joyously they met their problems and built decent, prosperous communities. "But suddenly," she concluded her first installment, at the very heyday of this confidence, "a big hand reached out from nobody knew where, to steal their conquest and throttle their future." John D. Rockefeller had arrived. (*See Reading No. 5.*)

Rockefeller. Tarbell said of Rockefeller that "to drive a good bargain was the joy of his life." Through diligent labor and efficiency, he and his associates ruthlessly took control of refining in nearby Cleveland. Their quietly-formed South Improvement Company entered into secret arrangements with the railroads for reduced freight rates. The other refiners couldn't compete and had to sell out at Rockefeller's price. In three months, Standard Oil "became master of over one-fifth of the refining capacity of the United States." Soon after, the railroads doubled the rate for shipping oil from the fields. However, Rockefeller was shipping so much oil that he could force almost anything he wanted out of the railroads which competed for his business. They secretly gave him a rebate of a dollar a barrel for the oil he shipped, plus a similar amount as a rake-off from the rates paid by competing shippers. The oil region rose in revolt. A Producers Council shut down production in the fields and sought aid from the Pennsylvania legislature. Seemingly brought to terms, Rockefeller agreed to buy at the producers' price. Then, when the Producers Council was dissolved and the wells pumping again, he cut his payments in half. Using his immense profits, he bought barrel factories, tank cars, terminal facilities, and companies in Pittsburgh, New York, Philadelphia, Cleveland, and the oil regions. He was shipping so much oil that the railroads kicked back what he asked and again raised the rates for oil shipped by other refiners.

Industrial War. Out of a sense of individualism and the "love of independent work," the oil men resisted. Mr. Rockefeller scorned such weak sentiment. Motivated by a love of profits alone, he pushed forward through "persuasion, intimidation, or force," toward his secret, relentless goal of monopoly. When competitors appeared, or the producers sought to build their own pipelines or refineries, Rockefeller bought them out or cut them down. Congressional investigations, legislative battles, bills for "free" pipelines and for regulation, and a war with the Pennsylvania Railroad's oil carrying Empire Transportation Company all resulted in victories for Standard Oil.

The producers continued to struggle against the leviathan, and Ida Tarbell's girlhood sympathies for the "little men" never waivered. In 1878, the independents managed to get Rockefeller and his associates indicted for conspiracy of monopoly and all of its injurious devices. But again the producers failed to stand firm. Standard was allowed to get off the hook with a compromise settlement, which it proceeded to violate. Having broken organized opposition, Rockefeller, as ever, moved to silence individual complaint. Another successful struggle enabled him to capture the independent's new pipeline to the eastern seaboard. With her collections of documents, reports, investigations, and ledgers, Ida Tarbell proceeded to show how Rockefeller moved from control of refining and transportation to take over marketing. Through efficiency, force, espionage, threats, and ruthless price-cutting by "bogus" companies, Standard continued to spread.

Having told the story of Standard's success, Ida Tarbell began to look even more deeply into its methods. Describing John D. Rockefeller's secrecy and the dread he inspired among the oil producers, she told the story of Standard's continued illegal rebates from the railroads, the mysterious explosion that destroyed a competing refinery in Buffalo, and the power of Standard in the Ohio and Pennsylvania legislatures. When finally a brave, young Attorney General of Ohio resisted intense pressure and brought the trust to court, the judges reduced the dissolution order to meaninglessness.

The Cost Was Too Great. In her concluding installments, Ida Tarbell summed up "the legitimate greatness" of Standard Oil, describing its energy, intelligence, organizational skill, genuis for detail, audacity, alertness, effectiveness, superior ability, and com-

mercial vision. But for Ida Tarbell, the cost was too great. It meant
high prices, illegal and unethical behavior, autocratic and ruthless
power, and the destruction of the free, independent, competitive life
of the oil fields. "Human experience long ago taught us," she argued,
"that if we allowed a man or a group of men autocratic powers in
government or church, they used that power to oppress and defraud
the public."

Success. The series was a smashing success. The accompanying
photographs and sketches (an art in which the popular magazines
excelled) were in themselves a technological history of the oil
industry. Tarbell's mastery of the details of Standard's affairs,
together with the use of names, dates, and statistics, supported by
reproductions of government reports and court records, seemed to
back up her tales of illegality and conspiracy. So did reproductions
of ledgers and correspondence which had been secretly supplied her
by sympathetic Standard Oil employees.

"The History of the Standard Oil Company" aroused the indignation of the reading public. It provided subject matter for cartoonists,
editorialists, indignant social gospel ministers who labeled Rockefeller's charitable donations as "tainted money," and political controversy. Reformers consulted her. While it would not be possible to
give Ida Tarbell direct credit for starting them, her writings focused
the attention on Standard Oil and created public support for some
twenty state anti-trust suits and the Bureau of Corporations
investigation that led to national government filing one also.

In her *History* and in two later character studies for *McClure's*,
Ida Tarbell made John D. Rockefeller the symbol of commercial
greed and corruption in America—"Commercial Machiavellianism," she called it. Mixing together the business tactics of the
Standard Oil Company and Rockefeller's own secretiveness and
commercial diligence, she created "the Rockefeller legend" of a man
consumed by the money passion and what a later generation would
see as puritan inner-directedness and greed. (*See Readings No. 6 and
7.*)

Ray Stannard Baker. Baker was the third of *McClure's* ground-
breaking trio of writers. In keeping with the popular interest in the
new industrial society, Baker had been writing about modern
business and businessmen such as U. S. Steel and J. P. Morgan. S. S.
McClure sent him off to have a look at a strike in the Pennsylvania
coal fields, and he produced a much-praised series on labor warfare

in America. Like Steffens and Tarbell, Baker's theme was individual-ism. The problem was lawlessness. To Lincoln Steffens individual-ism meant civic pride and an enduring concern for proper govern-ment. To Ida Tarbell it was the competitive owner-producers of the oil fields. For Baker, it was not letting the bosses control things.

Industrial Lawlessness. Baker's first labor article, "The Right to Work," described the hardships of the non-striking miners and their abuse at the hands of the strikers. It was illustrated by photographs of sad-faced workingmen and their families. In succeeding articles, Baker continued to hit the theme of individual effort, which brought him praise from President Roosevelt. Initially Baker criticized labor bosses and the combinations of labor and capital which squeezed the public. However, as he investigated the widespread violence in the Colorado minefields, he came to feel that the misdeeds of labor were not as great and as provocative as those of capital. Theodore Roosevelt called these accounts "absolutely correct and fair."

The theme that S. S. McClure used in his movement-making, January 1903, editorial was "lawlessness." Lincoln Steffens' politi-cians, Ida Tarbell's capitalists, and Ray Stannard Baker's working-men were all breaking the law and getting away with it. McClure's writers picked up his theme of lawlessness, but initially they used it to try to arouse civic pressure to get the laws enforced and lawbreakers punished. Gradually, with some confusion, the defini-tion of "lawlessness" shifted from law violations to a concern for controlling the power of giant corporations, for getting new regula-tions passed, and for doing something about the exploitation of the poor and less fortunate.

CHAPTER 4

The Power of Dollars

Frenzied Finance. As the new kind of journalism in *McClure's* captured popular interest, other magazine men drifted into it. Thomas W. Lawson came from outside and jumped in with both feet. His tempestuous "inside" revelations of stock market manipulations in "Frenzied Finance, The Crime of Amalgamated" was one of the most spectacular and least reliable contributions of the era. It was also the most talked about series of 1904. Lawson was a speculator. He specialized in organizing pools to manipulate stocks on the market and drew in large numbers of small investors through extravagant claims and publicity. He worked best when bearishly tearing down stock values and in one of his forays almost wrecked the General Electric Company. He had joined with the Standard Oil group in organizing an inflated trust in copper. They squeezed him out and he was furious. The editors of *Everybody's* found it easy to sign him up to "tell all."

Lawson's message was "the power of dollars." At no time in the history of the Republic had it been as great. With its banks, insurance companies, mines, manufactories, colleges, churches, and the power to influence the selection of the President of the United States, the "System" plundered the American people of millions. The heart of this money-stealing "System" was 26 Broadway, the home of the Standard Oil Company. The two prime operatives were the Rockefeller partner Henry H. Rogers and National City Bank President James Stillman.

Lawson offered a continuation of Ida Tarbell's story of John D. Rockefeller and the building of the Standard Oil Company. With John D. in virtual retirement, Lawson described the role of oil man H. H. Rogers and the expansion of Standard's power into the speculative control of other industries. He wrote about Standard Oil money and its allies on Wall Street, about its banks and insurance companies, its corruption of the courts, and its inside arrangements with legislators and other public officials. (*See Reading No. 8.*)

Juggling with Millions of the People's Money. Lawson revealed that the new field for conquest had been the copper industry, and the manipulators had put together a trust. The companies already in the field were forced in, bought out, or ruined. Initially the cost of the copper properties was to be $39,000,000. To raise this amount, the would-be monopolists issued $75,000,000 worth of stock, at a par value of $100 a share. They sold enough stock to pay for the properties while holding back a major portion of the stock for themselves. As the price soared up to $140 a share, they began to dump their enormous holdings on the market. When they had forced the price down to $75 a share (taking a big profit along the way), they bought it back again and were ready for a second go around.

Dollars, dollars, dollars, rang the theme of Lawson's articles. He charged that under the "Black Flag" of Wall Street, the financial buccaneers of the "System" were "juggling with millions of the people's money." From 1904 through 1907, Lawson's exposés ran in twenty monthly installments. Advertising rates eventually reached $500 a page. Soon subscriptions mounted to three-quarters of a million, and *Everybody's* was carrying more than 150 pages of advertising. Instead of receiving a fee, Lawson had asked *Everybody's* to spend $50,000 for advertising the series, and he claimed that he added to this with his own money. While circulation grew, Erman Ridgway and his editors debated the literary merits of such purple Lawsonian prose as the description of an angered H. H. Rogers sounding like "a rattlesnake's hiss in a refrigerator."

It was a sensation. Lawsuits and shootings were threatened. Conservative magazines muckraked Lawson, and Norman Hapgood, the reformist editor of *Collier's*, ran an editorial on "How Much of a Liar is Lawson?" While Hapgood lamented Lawson's financial morals, he predicted that he had "set in motion a force which will hardly stop short of serious reforms."

Life Insurance. The most direct result of Lawson's series was one he had not anticipated. In an early installment, he mentioned the use of insurance company funds as part of the "System's" power, and he singled out the New York Life Insurance Company by name. This brought a flood of letters from readers. Soon the special "Questions and Answers" section, "Lawson and Critics," was devoted to his promises to "cause a life-insurance blaze." (*See Reading No. 9.*)

The kindling was already alight within the industry. In the growth and consolidations of the latter part of the nineteenth century, Mutual, Equitable, and New York Life had emerged as the nation's largest insurance companies. An internal power struggle going on within Equitable broke into the press. An elegant costume ball thrown by Henry Hyde, the founder's high-living son, and paid for by the company, was sensationally described and denounced by Joseph Pulitzer's New York *World*. Young Hyde was only a birthday away from inheriting his father's controlling stock in Equitable. The leading officers of the company were out to prevent this, even at the cost of making Equitable a mutual company and sharing the profits with the policy holders. The New York *World* kept the story in the open, as the financial tycoons E. H. Harriman, Henry Clay Frick, Thomas F. Ryan, and J. P. Morgan competed for control of the company.

By law, the income from young Hyde's stock was limited to a grand total of $3,524 a year, but offers for it had gone as high as seven million dollars. Obviously the power to manage Equitable's half billion dollar assets was of considerable value. Lawson joined in the brawl that he had unintentionally helped publicize, although it was the New York *World's* dogged reporting and editorials which finally led the New York State legislature to set up an investigating committee.

Questioning by the Armstrong Committee counsel Charles Evans Hughes revealed the high salaries paid to company executives and their families, the risky investments and the private speculations with the policy holders' funds, the hidden bank accounts, and the secret contributions to the national political parties. The insurance companies had even kept a special residence in Albany, dubbed by the press as "The House of Mirth," where they paid off state legislators. All told, the companies had juggled their books to conceal discrepancies of millions. Some of the money was refunded; the old officers departed, and most of the companies were turned into policy holders mutuals—though without much increase of participation in management. The New York legislature passed a series of regulatory laws which were copied by other states. The new management disengaged the companies from Wall Street's "high finance" operations. Charles Evans Hughes became Governor, almost President, and later the U. S. Supreme Court's Chief Justice.

Lawson's Return to Finance. Although Thomas Lawson continued to crow and claim credit for it all, he offered no constructive suggestions for change. The Committee counsel, Hughes, had not deemed it useful to seek his testimony, and Lawson did not seem to have offered it. He understood life insurance funds, perhaps too well, and it was difficult to tell whether his campaign for insurance company proxies in the fall of 1905 was to correct or take advantage of the situation. The financial lawyer, Samuel Untermeyer, who was later to head a congressional investigation of Wall Street (Pujo Committee, 1912–1913), handled Lawson's proxy campaign. Probably not even Lawson himself could tell where the line could be drawn between public enlightenment and his own gain and revenge.

Even while he was writing "Frenzied Finance," he had continued to play the market. In 1907, he announced that he was abandoning his public and returning to finance. "What do I owe to the gelatine-spined shrimps?" he wrote to Ridgway. Five years later he reappeared in *Everybody's* to belatedly offer "The Remedy" of federal regulation of the stock exchange and the reduction of capitalization to actual assets. Although Henry Ashurst of Arizona introduced it as a bill in the United States Senate, it generated little interest, either in that body or among the reading public.

Burton J. Hendrick. It remained for Burton Jesse Hendrick to soberly sum up "The Story of Life Insurance" in a six-part series for *McClure's* the next year. Hendrick became the muckraker biographer of the great American fortunes, particularly of the traction (street railway) and railroad magnates. He disliked the weak and avaricious and feared organized labor, but he admired the men of strength and particularly idolized Charles Evans Hughes. After his muckrake years, Hendrick was to win two Pulitzer Prizes for biography in the 1920s.

Hendrick told the life insurance story straight, presenting perhaps the best general public summary of what Hughes and the Armstrong Committee had discovered. The history of the insurance industry over the preceding thirty-five years had been one of progressive degeneracy. The companies had turned themselves into speculative syndicates, changing their emphasis from life insurance to financial enterprize. (*See Reading No. 10.*) Even when they were not engaged in extravagance or dishonesty, the insurance magnates invested their policy holders' money poorly.

By the turn of the century, the United States had become the world's leading industrial nation. Wall Street, down near the tip of Manhattan Island, with its stock exchange and its big banking houses, was the national money market. Tom Lawson's role, whatever his motives, was to sound alarm about the financial manipulations made possible by such a spectacular concentration of money and power. Public interest focused on the great insurance companies. Lawson's hot prose helped touch off a state investigation of the insurance industry, whose practices Burton Hendrick later coolly recorded for the magazine public. The Armstrong Committee and the New York legislature produced an extensive set of controls, which other states copied. It was not until 1944 that the U.S. Supreme Court ruled that insurance was an interstate business and subject to national regulation. State supervision, led by New York, had worked sufficiently well to keep the industry healthy when most of the rest of the national business structure collapsed during the great depression of the 1930s.

The problems of the "money monopoly" and the weaknesses of the stock market and the national banking and credit system had become a central progressive era political issue. A congressional investigation by the Pujo Committee in 1912 produced graphic details about a "money trust." Woodrow Wilson's election as President in that year was in part due to concern over what he called the "dangerously concentrated" control of wealth. The Federal Reserve System (1913) was a partial step in the direction of doing something about the problem. The great stock market crash of 1929, the depression of the 1930s, and the continuing instability of the economy indicate that while muckraking had helped highlight a central economic problem, solutions were complex and incomplete.

CHAPTER 5

Poison: Meat and Drugs

A New *Uncle Tom's Cabin.* The young socialist novelist Upton Sinclair argued that only authors knew enough to review their own books. Writing in 1906 about his spectacular new novel *The Jungle*, he called it a "New *Uncle Tom's Cabin*," and he wasn't far from wrong. In many ways his novel of the Chicago packing houses may have contributed as much to the emergence of the national regulation of business as Harriet Beecher Stowe's novel did to bring on the Civil War.

President Theodore Roosevelt was greatly concerned that the greed and corruption in politics was causing a dangerous popular unrest. He felt that if it were not checked it might lead to the socialism preached by "hysterical" men such as Sinclair. Roosevelt's solution was the regulation of business by the national government.

The Limitations of the Presidency. At the beginning of 1906, the prospect of government regulation of business did not seem very likely. A conservative Congress, operating under an undemocratic set of rules and traditions, influenced by business interests, and often confined by constitutional scruples, was little interested in change. The President used his executive powers to do what he could, intervening in coal strikes and bringing anti-trust suits against big monopolies and railroad combinations. T. R. used his office as a "Bully Pulpit" to educate the public, but national regulatory legislation depended on an unenthusiastic Congress. However, before the summer of 1906 was over, the government had gained regulatory power over the railroads, the packing houses, and the food and drug industries. Roosevelt was mainly responsible for having gotten the laws passed although he had dedicated help from some congressmen and senators. The constitutional authority rested on the interstate commerce clause. Public support had in good part been generated by the muckrakers and the press.

The Battle over Patent Medicines. The muckrakers' historian, Louis Filler, has described the battle over patent medicines as the product of a coming together of science, politics, and literature. The battle began over the "patent medicines." Men have long believed that mysterious remedies exist which would be good for whatever ails them. The more secret the ingredients and the greater the promises, the better. Such wondrous nostrums came to be called "patent" or "proprietary" medicines. Druggists as well as traveling men sold them. The historian James Harvey Young claims that patent medicines became the first American brand-name products to take advantage of the national market that the railroads and a growing magazine-reading public made possible. The "medical messiahs" and "toadstool millionaires" pioneered in national advertising after the Civil War and became its top spenders. Whether the problem was a woman's ailment, a crying child, cold, cough, or catarrh, rheumatism, sluggishness, or cancer, *Lydia Pinkham, Peruna, Paine's Celery Compound, Burdock's Blood Bitters, Doctor Pierce's Favorite Prescription,* or *Colden's Liquid Beef Tonic* had a pill, salve, or tonic for it. The chances were that the vital secret ingredient was alcohol, opium, or the powerful heart stimulant, Digitalis, liberally mixed with water, flavor, and coloring.

The census of 1900 reported a patent medicine income of some $59,000,000. It was later estimated that more money went for advertising than for either production or profit. Contracts with newspapers and magazines provided for cancellation of advertising if individual states should pass laws, or if newspapers carried adverse reports on the nostrums.

Nevertheless, opposition began to mount. Some newspapers refused to accept advertising for the medicines, and in 1892 Edward Bok, editor of the influential *Ladies Home Journal*, announced that it was closing its pages to the patent medicines. The American Medical Association, the American Pharmaceutical Association, and some state chemists joined the opposition. Harvey Wiley, the dynamic chief chemist of the Department of Agriculture took up the battle against the harmful and secret nostrums and preservatives. In 1904, the journals brought the issue to a focus. *The Ladies Home Journal* was never to become a muckraking magazine and *Collier's Weekly* had not yet joined, but together they produced 1905s second major sensation. If the spring and summer belonged to life insurance, the fall witnessed the crusade against the poison purveyors.

The Ladies Home Journal and Mark Sullivan. In a 1904 editorial on patent medicines, Edward Bok listed the harmful contents of a number of popular nostrums. His information was wrong about *Dr. Pierce's Favorite Prescription* and *The Ladies Home Journal* had to print a retraction and pay damages. To prevent any more such costly mishaps, Bok hired the young lawyer-journalist Mark Sullivan to gather and check facts for future efforts. Sullivan turned out to be a good detective. He interviewed patent medicine company employees, secured the secret minutes of the manufacturers' trade association meetings and copies of the "muzzling" contracts with the press. Soon Sullivan had learned most of the tricks of the trade. There was one coup of which he was particularly proud. In the advertisements for Lydia Pinkham's remedies, women were urged to write to her at her laboratory for personal advice—Sullivan discovered that she had been dead for more than twenty years. He took a picture of the gravestone, and *The Ladies Home Journal* published it alongside of the advertisement.

When Sullivan summed up his findings on how the manufacturers used their advertising contracts, it was too long for the *Journal*. Bok sold it to Norman Hapgood at *Collier's Weekly*, who published it under the title "The Patent Medicine Conspiracy Against Freedom of the Press." *Collier's* had recently entered the anti-corruption crusade because of an argument with William Jennings Bryan over the patent medicine advertisements. Although Bryan's newspaper, *The Commoner*, attacked the misbehavior of big business, it ran full page patent medicine ads. When *Collier's* pointed out this inconsistency, Bryan wrote resentfully to the editor.

Collier's and Samuel Hopkins Adams. After running Sullivan's article, *Collier's* editor Hapgood hired Samuel Hopkins Adams, who had written some good health articles for *McClure's*, to expose the patent medicine industry. After an editorial build-up and some great cartoons, including one by E. W. Kemble of a death's head with patent medicine bottles as teeth, Adams began a year-long series on "The Great American Fraud." The American people, Adams reported, were spending $75,000,000 a year for supposed medicines which were in reality alcohol, opiates, narcotics, dangerous depressants and stimulants, and undiluted fraud. (*See Reading No. 11.*)

As Adams pounded away sensationally at the fakes and the

poisons, Theodore Roosevelt called for legislation. In his annual
message to Congress in December of 1905, the President asked for a
"law to be enacted to regulate interstate commerce in misbranded
and adulterated foods, drinks, and drugs." Such a law had been
proposed in Congress for several years. Bills had passed the House
of Representatives twice, but the manufacturers and much of the
nation's press fought them and regulation never reached a vote in
the Senate. However, the magazines had stirred up a tempest. The
President joined with the American Medical Association, the
Women's Christian Temperance Union, the National Consumers'
League, the General Federation of Women's Clubs, and the tireless
government chemist, Harvey Wiley, in the fight.

Upton Sinclair and *The Jungle*. In 1906, a bill to regulate the
industries had passed the Senate but was dying in the House, when
an explosion took place. After having been turned down by some
four or five other publishers, Upton Sinclair's book on the packing
houses, *The Jungle*, was published by Doubleday, Page & Company
early in 1906. Despite adverse literary comment, it burst into the
headlines. Within weeks it had sold 25,000 copies and created an
almost irresistible public demand for meat inspection. Driven by
poverty, ill-health, a failed youthful marriage, and a sense of his
destiny as a writer, the young Sinclair had moved to socialism from
the clichés of literary naturalism. With the publication of his book
he became an evangelist. Unlike the other journalists, his motivation
was ideological. The socialist paper, *Appeal to Reason*, had sent him
to investigate the oppression of labor in the Chicago meatpack-
ing industry, and Sinclair turned the report into a documentary
novel.

The Jungle was a first rate piece of writing. The novel told the
story of the dark-haired, powerful young giant, Jurgis, and his fair,
blue-eyed young bride, Ona, who were part of an extended
Lithuanian family immigration to America. After the wedding feast,
the real theme of the story emerged as Jurgis, in search of a job,
viewed the magnificently efficient organization of the slaughter-
house. As the hogs entered, they were chained by the leg, hooked to
a wheel and jerked aloft along an overhead trolley, kicking and
squealing, throats split, blood flowing and then ebbing as the
carcasses were carried into vats of boiling water. "Dieve—but I'm
glad I'm not a hog!" muttered Jurgis. But he was. Against a
panoramic depiction of Chicago, the packing and harvester plants,

the street railways, the slums, prostitution, the tramps, the saloons, beggary, crime, gambling, and the world of politically organized graft, vice, corruption, and protected wealth, Jurgis and his family were hooked on to a slaughterhouse trolley, cut to pieces, and scraped as clean of humanity as any squealing pig. In the end, with the family gone and only the reduced hulk of Jurgis left, the Socialist Party stepped in to offer redemption.

The Stomach of the Nation. *The Jungle* was a grimly depressing book. It would have been a hardened reader who was not moved by the human misery and despair which Sinclair chronicled. However, public attention focused on the processing of meat, not the processing of the workers and their families. The outcry rose over accounts of corrupt inspectors and tubercular beef and over old meat, mouldy and dosed with borax and glycerine, and over rats and poisoned bread set out for them, all of which were mixed in with the carcasses of goats and horses. (*See Reading No. 12.*) On occasion, the dinner table product was even flavored with workmen who fell into the vats and had "all but the bones of them" go "out to the world as Durham's Pure Leaf Lard." Perhaps the whole picture was too much for the mind and the heart to handle. Perhaps the middle-class readers were not prepared for a call to overturn the system and had to find a more limited evil to which to react. Perhaps the shock of the food handling was all it could take. At any rate, Sinclair wrote later that year that "I aimed at the public's heart, and by accident I hit it in the stomach."

It was a powerful blow, and the meat packers were particularly vulnerable. The scandal of "embalmed beef" supplied to the soldiers during the war with Spain was still remembered. A distinguished British medical journal, *The Lancet*, had already attacked the Chicago packing houses, and so had Samuel Merwin in *Success Magazine*. Out of the government price-fixing suit against Swift and Company and the anti-trust suit against Armour and the other packers, the able newsman Charles Edward Russell had written an eight-part series in *Everybody's* titled "The Greatest Trust in the World."

Theodore Roosevelt. Sinclair sent a copy of *The Jungle* to President Roosevelt, whose Commissioner of Corporations brought him another. Frank Doubleday sent the President the proofs of three authoritative articles that were to appear in *World's Work*. Roosevelt was scornful of Sinclair's socialism as well as of the meat packer's greed, but he met with Sinclair and promised to investigate. Although the Agriculture Department upheld the packers, a special investigatory team composed of the Commissioner of Labor and a New York social worker reported to the President that conditions in the meat industry were very bad. The press, both at home and in Europe, picked up the cry. Europeans were concerned that meat sent abroad was so poorly inspected; the American newspapers complained that meat intended for the domestic market was not checked at all. Upton Sinclair bombarded both the press and the President with calls and letters. The Administration was preparing a meat inspection bill, and the President's increasingly reformist friend Indiana Senator Albert J. Beveridge took up the fight in Congress after reading *The Jungle*. The packers fought regulation, using the Chicago *Tribune* and the *Saturday Evening Post* to deny all charges. When the packers continued to resist, President Roosevelt released the report of his investigators, most of which Sinclair had already leaked to the press, and worked skillfully for the passage of the law.

The Meat Inspection Act. The poisoning of the meat-eating public was the leading topic of the day (*see Reading No. 13*), and the New York *Evening Post* summed up the feeling in a little jingle:

> Mary had a little lamb
> And when she saw it sicken,
> She shipped it off to Packingtown
> And now it's labeled chicken.

Although the packers desperately needed to improve their reputation by accepting some sort of reform, they resisted even the mild regulation proposed in Congress. After a bitter battle, a somewhat adulterated Meat Inspection Act was passed in 1906, and the furor over this issue helped carry the Pure Food and Drug Law as well. The meat inspection law provided for a somewhat tightened system of inspection of meat destined for interstate markets, as well as abroad. Local production remained under state jurisdiction and did not yield to national control until sixty years later. When President Lyndon Johnson signed the extension in 1967, Upton Sinclair was present as an honored guest but made no mention of socialist revolution.

The Pure Food and Drug Act. The Pure Food and Drug law when finally enacted in 1906 was a similarly watered-down measure.

Harmful ingredients such as alcohol and drugs had to be identified on the labels, but disclosure of other elements was not required. Any false information was punishable. Although the journalists were concerned only about patent medicines, the fight had been a broader one. Led by government chemist Dr. Harvey Wiley, the backers of the law were concerned with the general problem of food adulteration, including that of the whiskey industry. Of the successful cases during the law's first five years, only ten percent dealt with the proprietary medicines. The American Medical Association created a special Associate Fellowship for Samuel Hopkins Adams and circulated a reprint of his "Great American Fraud" in what may have been hundreds of thousands of copies. Nevertheless, within a few years, Adams was writing that the government and the courts were "poisoning" the law by their refusal to vigorously carry out and uphold it. The problem of effective administration is as old as the history of the regulatory state itself; in practice, a law is seldom better than the way it is enforced.

CHAPTER **6**

The Railroads

The Modern Decline of the Railroads. In the 1960s the economic historian Robert Fogel calculated that the railroads' share in the growth of America had been greatly overrated by previous histori- ans. In the 1970s the railroads had fallen to such a low estate that former astronaut Wally Schirra was hired to soothingly intone over the television, "The American Railroads: Who needs them? You do." Two of the great eastern trunk railroads were merged into the Penn-Central, in an operation that Theodore Roosevelt would never have let pass by, and then brought to bankruptcy by the kind of insider-manipulation that formed the chief grist for the journalistic mills of the Progressive Era. However, in 1970 when the national government organized a nation-wide passenger system merger, there were no loud outcries of either "monopoly" or "socialism."

The Centrality of the Railroads in 1900. Throughout the nineteenth century the American railroad system had pushed to the West Coast and helped to populate the continent. It had been the greatest user of steel, labor, and investment capital. The Thomas Scotts, Grenville Dodges, and James J. Hills had built it. The William Vanderbilts and E. H. Harrimans helped reorganize it. The Jay Goulds looted it, and the J. P. Morgans sought to consolidate it. The railroads helped create a national market. The Grangers, Farmers' Alliancemen, and Populists blamed their troubles on railroad charges and discrimination, and it was generally believed that what the railroads did was crucial for business, the consumers, and the national economy.

According to Ida Tarbell, the secret of Standard Oil's success had been control over transportation. Standard became big enough to force the railroads to charge it less than its competitors. With kickbacks from the railroads (rebates and drawbacks), Standard grew even larger, destroyed more competitors, and demanded bigger rebates and drawbacks. "Until the people of the United States have solved the question of free and equal transportation," she wrote, "it is idle to suppose that they will not have a trust question."

Charles Edward Russell and the Power of the Railroads. The same assumption underlay the writing of many other popular journalists. Charles Edward Russell learned the lesson early. He had inherited his anti-tariff and anti-railroad views from his father, an anti-slavery newspaper editor in Davenport, Iowa. Russell's friend, James Baird Weaver, the perennial Greenback candidate, taught him that corporate power over transportation was the greatest menace to the Republic. Russell's father fought the growing power of the railroads and lost his paper to them. Though Russell became a successful big city newspaper man and an editor and publisher in the Hearst system, he retained his hostility. Control over transportation, he believed, lay at the root of the trust problem, and this concern over trusts, slums, and "the surplus" eventually led him into the Socialist Party.

In the summer of 1905, the government was presenting its case against the meat packers for controlling the prices which they paid the cattle raisers and which they charged the consumers. *Everybody's* persuaded Russell to cover the proceedings and launched him on a career as a journalist of exposure. In less than a decade, Russell produced more than 150 articles, many of them later reprinted in book form, and became a socialist. He wrote eight articles on the beef trust, arguing that railroad favoritism had helped create "The Greatest Trust in the World." The packers controlled stockyards, factories, legislators, and the price people paid for their daily food. "Three times a day," Russell wrote, "this power comes to the table of every household in America." Basically the problem was the profit motive, whose "money getting mania" produced inequalities, fortunes, and trust conditions.

The Case for Government Ownership. In late 1905, *Everybody's* sent Russell abroad to see how other countries were making out. The trip supplied a three-year series of articles. In "Soldiers of the Common Good" (reprinted as *The Uprising of the Many* in 1907), Russell confirmed his previous conclusions. Private control of transportation and private profit were the heart of the problem. The results were "privilege, caste, class, corruption, great wealth in the hands of a few, the idea that wealth is immune from the law," the growth of the slums, the spread of disease, and the destruction of democracy. Russell's solution was not national regulation but governmental ownership of transportation. The government had to "operate the Trust for the Common Good instead of for private gain." The growing power of Germany and Japan and the development of a more complete democracy in Australia and New Zealand were based on public control of "the national highways for national use." (*See Reading No. 14.*) During the years that followed, Russell repeated his arguments about transportation, trusts, and public ownership in articles for *Cosmopolitan, Hearst's, Success,* and *Hampton's.*

Russell's proposal for government ownership was further than Theodore Roosevelt and most of the American people seemed interested in going. Although Roosevelt had made the first successful use of the Sherman Anti-trust Act, his goal was national regulation, not breaking up the trusts. "On the interstate commerce business, which I regard as a matter of principle," the President stated, "I shall fight."

Ray Stannard Baker. By 1905, the time of Russell's initial railroad series, Ray Stannard Baker had also come to believe that railroad favoritism was the chief cause of monopoly power. He too was soon to go beyond seeking regulation. In his series on "Railroads on Trial" in *McClure's,* which paralleled the President's own regulatory campaign, Baker saw himself engaged in a crusade against special privilege. The more he delved into the subject, the angrier he became. The railroads not only built monopolies and taxed the consumers, but they also determined the economic life and death of communities. In writing of "The Way of a Railroad with a Town," he showed how the Southern Railway's discriminatory rates meant prosperity to Lynchburg, Virginia, and hard times for neighboring Danville. (*See Reading No. 15.*) Regulation was necessary, but through a gigantic system of publicity, pressure, and misinformation the carriers manipulated newspapers and public opinion and utilized corrupt bosses and legislatures.

Harvard Professor W. Z. Ripley, a top railroad expert, wrote in praise of Baker's series as did one of the members of the Interstate Commerce Commission. The most satisfying comment came from the White House. "I haven't a criticism to suggest . . ." the President wrote on seeing proofs of one of the articles, "You have given me two or three thoughts for my own message." Their correspondence continued and Roosevelt sent Baker the galleys of his own forthcoming annual message to Congress.

Baker argued that the Interstate Commerce Commission needed power to set minimum rates as well as maximum ones if discrimination were to be prevented. Roosevelt was playing a wily political game with a conservative Congress, and felt that that would have to come later. Both Baker and the President saw a rising tide of radicalism. Both felt that unless an effective regulatory bill were passed, government ownership would be inevitable. By the spring of 1906, as the Congressional battle heated, Baker had come to believe that government ownership might be a good thing. It was no more confiscatory, he wrote, than for the railroads to take the people's property by unfair levies. During a conversation with Baker, the President asked, "If this [regulatory bill] is only a first step where do you think we are going?" "You may not agree with me, Mr. President," Baker replied, "but I believe we cannot stop short of governmental ownership of the railroads."

For the next several years, Baker edged closer to socialism, confining his thoughts primarily to his private journal. Charles Edward Russell marched boldly toward it, finally joining the Socialist Party in 1908, the year in which Baker decided to pull back. While keeping President Roosevelt's friendship, Baker developed warm ties with Senator Robert M. La Follette of Wisconsin, who seemed willing to go further in the direction of national regulation than Roosevelt among the reform-minded leaders whom Baker termed the "progressive party."

Theodore Roosevelt and Regulation. Theodore Roosevelt respected Ray Stannard Baker, took him into his confidence, and apparently used him as an intellectual sparring partner in preparing for the railroad regulation bout with the Congress in 1906. The President gave little sign of interest in the articles of Charles Edward Russell, whose accuracy and growing radicalism he came to distrust. As for David Graham Phillips, the President relegated him to the most condemned category of hades, as one of those hysterically untrustworthy sensationalists who were doing so much to stir up the dangerously extremist popular mood. Nevertheless, the President needed all the help he could get during the congressional battle. Phillips' well wrought depiction of the connection between the railroads, bossism, and corruption in his novel *The Plum Tree* (1905) and in his luridly presented "Treason of the Senate" in the spring of 1906, probably helped get the law through Congress.

The Hepburn Act, passed during the summer of 1906, made railroad regulation reasonably effective for the first time. The Interstate Commerce Commission, created in 1887 as the first national agency for regulating business, now had its supervision extended to terminal and storage facilities, sleeping and refrigerator cars, pipelines, ferries, and bridges. When a railroad charge was contested, the Commission could set its own more "reasonable" maximum rate. The railroads could no longer give free passes to influence their "friends," and the Commission could tell the railroad companies how to keep their books. If a railroad disagreed with Commission actions, it had to carry the burden of proof. In short, the ICC was given broader supervision, control of the books, and the right to change maximum rates.

Although the ICC was strengthened, the railroad problem was not settled. Capitalization, service, and labor relations were among the problems which remained. For the next half decade, journalists such as Will Irwin, C. P. Connolly, Burton Hendrick, G. K. Turner, and Lincoln Steffens continued to catalogue and damn railroad misbehavior and power on the pages of *Collier's, McClure's* and *Everybody's*. Both President Roosevelt and President William Howard Taft called for additional legislation. However, if the Hepburn Act of 1906 was the high point of Theodore Roosevelt's regulatory achievement and of his skillful political leadership of Congress, the journalists whom he called "muckrakers" played a prominent and useful part.

The revitalized Interstate Commerce Commission became the prime model for the American regulatory capitalist system. The underlying assumptions were restriction and competition. The railroads must not discriminate between customers, but should compete among themselves. The government would prohibit wrong behavior, but it was not responsible for helping railroads solve their problems and for guiding an overall national railroad system. In the 1900s, no one envisioned a transportation world dominated by cars, trucks, tankers, pipelines, and airplanes. The railroads were king, and what the reformers demanded of them was that they behave like constitutional monarchs, not absolute rulers and tyrants.

CHAPTER 7

Treason, Conservation and National Politics

One day in 1905, Charles Edward Russell later remembered, he had gone to the Senate press gallery. Beneath him in the chamber were "a row of well-fed and portly gentlemen, everyone of whom, we knew perfectly well, was there to represent some private (and predatory) Interest." The image in his mind must have been similar to a Joseph Keppler cartoon in *Puck* or *Judge* or one of Frederick B. Opper's in the New York *American*, in which bulging men with dollar-signs on their suits ran the nation. Russell considered doing a series on how the Senate served as a "chamber of butlers for industrialists and financiers."

William Randolph Hearst liked Russell's idea. Himself a congressman, Hearst had just bought *Cosmopolitan Magazine*. He was ready to use it, as he did his newspapers, to erratically and sensationally fuel a mass discontent which might well carry him into the White House. However, Russell went off on a round-the-world inspection of social unrest for *Everybody's*, and so *Cosmopolitan* settled on a polished young reporter-novelist named David Graham Phillips. Gustavus Myers, the student of Tammany Hall, and Phillips' brother, Harrison, were to do basic research.

David Graham Phillips. Phillips had followed the political trail of greed and wealth in his popular novels. In *The Plum Tree* (1905) serialized in *Success*, he fictionally surveyed the Senate of the United States. At the height of interest in "exposure," with *Cosmopolitan* drumming up a national audience, he had a chance to have a real go at that body. In many ways, the Senate was a proper target. At that time, Senators were elected by state legislatures, not by direct, popular vote. The campaign to change this, which was to result in

43

the Seventeenth Amendment to the Constitution in 1913, had long been underway and was then reaching the party platforms.

It was repeatedly charged and sometimes proven that bribery greased the way into the Senate. On occasion, when rich men contended, legislatures were unable to decide at all, and it was not unusual for seats to remain vacant, sometimes for years. The Senate was a rich man's club. It was said with some accuracy, that while there were no more than twenty millionaires in the whole United States in 1840, there were more than that in the United States Senate by the end of the century. During 1905, Senators from Oregon and Kansas were convicted on land and postal fraud charges, and others were under indictment. When Theodore Roosevelt sought business regulation, the Senate was the chief obstacle.

The Treason of the Senate. In February of 1906, the much heralded first installment of Phillips' "The Treason of the Senate" appeared. There were to be nine altogether, each beginning with the constitutional definition:

> Treason against the United States shall consist only in levying war against them, or in *adhering to their enemies, giving them aid and comfort.* (Constitution of the United States, Article III, Section 3)

Cosmopolitan's circulation increased fifty percent, and the newspaper reprint sales flourished. Phillips lambasted some nineteen senators by name and most of the rest by implication. "A man cannot serve two masters," he wrote; "The Senators are not elected by the people; they are elected by the 'interests.' "

The New York Central Railroad's man in the Senate was "Misrepresentative" Chauncey Depew. He was paid director's fees by more than seventy companies. He was, Phillips concluded, a servile instrument of the plutocracy. Senator Nelson Aldrich of Rhode Island was the "organizer" of the "treason." (*See Reading No. 16.*) Senator Arthur P. Gorman of Maryland, the Democratic minority leader, was his right hand man. Each of the others played a role in the great "merger" by which the "interests" ruled. Corrupted by purchase or association, the Senators controlled the distribution of wealth in America by helping their friends and masters, and by preventing any meaningful regulatory legislation. Altogether, before the abrupt end of the series in November, Phillips presented his case against Senators Chauncey Depew (R., N.Y.), Nelson W. Aldrich

(R., R.I.), Arthur P. Gorman (D., Md.), John C. Spooner (R., Wisc.), Joseph W. Bailey (D., Texas), Stephen B. Elkins (R., W. Va.), Shelby M. Cullom (R., Ill.), William B. Allison (R., Iowa), Philander C. Knox (R., Pa.), Joseph B. Foraker (R., Ohio), Henry Cabot Lodge (R., Mass.), Winthrop M. Crane (R., Mass.), John Kean (R., N.J.), William J. Stone (D., Mo.), Knute Nelson (R., Minn.), Moses Clapp (R., Minn.), Eugene Hale (R., Me.), William P. Fry (R., Me.), and Vice President-elect Charles W. Fairbanks (R., Ind.).

A Bitter Reaction. With the appearance of the initial article, the attack against Phillips mounted quickly. No single series and no writer, even Thomas Lawson, was as widely and bitterly criticized. Theodore Roosevelt took the lead. The President had difficulty in believing that any man employed by William Randolph Hearst to judge other men, could be anything but dishonest himself. To *Saturday Evening Post* editor George H. Lorimer, Roosevelt wrote that he did not believe that the treason articles could "do anything but harm." "They contain so much more falsehood than truth," he continued, "that they give no accurate guide for those who are really anxious to war against corruption, and they do excite a hysterical and ignorant feeling against everything existing." It was "the kind of hysteria," he said, using his favorite descriptive word for the journalists, that had produced the Terror of the French Revolution and made it "so difficult for the genuine reformers in Russia to secure reform in the teeth of those who mix up reform and destruction."

Roosevelt Coins a Name. The words that Phillips used most to describe the Senate were "interests" and "merger." In private, Roosevelt frequently used the epithet "hysterical" to refer to the journalistic style of the day. He first tried out the term "Muck-rake" at the annual "off-the-record" Gridiron Club dinner of the Washington newspapermen. Word spread and the response was most favorable, so Roosevelt decided to do it properly. A month later, in April of 1906, he repeated his message in public at the cornerstone laying of the new House of Representatives Office Building. (*See Reading No. 17.*)

It was a good speech, and a typical Rooseveltian argument against both ends of the spectrum, in which he reserved the middle for himself. "The men with the muck rakes" were "often indispensable to the well-being of society, but only if they know when to stop raking the muck, and to look upward to the celestial crown above them, to the crown of worthy endeavor." He argued that any excess of mudslinging was sure to promote reaction. Violent emotionalism and hysterical sensationalism excited unrest and "a foul class feeling" which frustrated constructive reform. Evil should be relentlessly uncovered, but "if the whole picture is painted black there remains no hue whereby to single out the rascals for distinction from their fellows." Dishonesty in public servants and corporations alike had to be rooted out. Problems such as "corruption," "the amassing of enormous fortunes," and "the far-reaching evils of over-capitalization" needed to be solved in order to produce "a broader economic opportunity" and promote "high individual character." The President warned that if the "men of wealth" succeeded in preventing proper public regulation of their business, they would provoke "the violent excesses which accompany a reform coming by convulsion instead of by steady and natural growth."

In his speech Roosevelt proposed a national progressive inheritance tax and supervision of corporations engaged in interstate commerce. However, it was the picture of the "Man with the Muck-rake" which caught public attention. The journalists of exposure had a name, and they didn't much like it.

In many ways the President's criticisms were justified. Much of the "muckrake" writing was missing the hues and painting the whole picture black. Motivation was complex, and not all rich men were corrupt. Many charges were too general and went too far. The President was probably not far off in privately likening Tom Lawson to a pickpocket who was trying to start "a panic in a theatre for the purpose of picking pockets in the rush." Even William Randolph Hearst found the "Treason of the Senate" articles short on documentation. Had Phillips applied the constitutional standard for treason, which required "the Testimony of two Witnesses to the same overt Act, or on Confession in open Court," little of his "evidence" would have survived.

The Treason and the Muck. Two historians of the Progressive era, George Mowry and Judson Grenier were to write more than half a century later that "Phillips's intemperate idiom is no longer considered good journalistic style, but the questions of public morality he raised remain." The muck was there and it would be difficult to disagree with Phillips' argument that the use of public office to plunder rather than serve the people was what treason was all about. As Lincoln Steffens wrote in "The Struggle for Self-Government," the politicians were organizing social treason by betraying the people whose trust they carried.

Despite their new label, 1906 was a potent year for the muckrakers. Probably none of them really mourned Hearst's loss to Charles Evans Hughes in the contest for the New York governorship that fall. They had helped produce the life insurance investigations that made Hughes a public figure and undoubtedly they contributed to the passage of the railroad, meat inspection, and pure food and drug laws that summer. The cry for political reform and for a change in the Senate was increasingly loud. But something was wrong.

The Impact of the Presidential Attack. President Roosevelt assured Ray Stannard Baker and Lincoln Steffens that he did not mean them (although he later privately included Steffens among the unreliables). When Norman Hapgood, the highly respected editor of *Collier's*, drew a distinction between the conscientious work of writers like Miss Tarbell, Lincoln Steffens and Ray Stannard Baker and the "distortion" and "shriek of accusations" of Phillips' writing, Phillips was terribly upset. So were many of the other journalists. Muckraking had begun in 1903 with S. S. McClure's recognition that a new kind of journalism was underway. In 1906 it reached a seeming high point in political impact with some of its most influential writing on food, drugs, the railroads, and the United States Senate. It had received its most severe criticism and its name, "muckraking," from President Roosevelt, whom the journalists had admired and undoubtedly helped politically. Perhaps, as a number of contemporary critics wrote, the American people were becoming tired of exposés. The tone of much of their writing had certainly become shrill. This was particularly true of Tom Lawson's accounts of Wall Street, Upton Sinclair's attack on the meat packers, and David Graham Phillips' indictment of the Senate. By 1906 it had become a profession, if not a movement. Able writers, mainly from the newspapers, continued to join. They were no longer surprised discoverers of corruption, but they still felt that there were reputations to make and conditions to change.

A New Phase. The original wielders of the muckrake, however, were in the process of change. They had been disturbed by the President's attack and were increasingly concerned, in T. R.'s phrase, with showing "more sky" in their writing. *McClure's Magazine* was in a state of crisis of another sort. The dynamic S. S. McClure was dreaming of speculative expansion into banks, life insurance companies, a university, and new publishing ventures. Office relationships were worsening. A group including Ida Tarbell, Ray Stannard Baker, Lincoln Steffens, William Allen White, the satirist Peter Finely Dunne, and several of the most talented editors bought *Leslie's Monthly Magazine* which they renamed the *American Magazine.* It was, they determined, going to be a journal of "uplift," looking for the hopeful as well as the underside of society.

The New Team on *McClure's*: Burton J. Hendrick. Although it was in a new phase, the age of political muckraking was far from over. Yale man and former New York *Evening Post* reporter Burton J. Hendrick took over the big business beat for *McClure's.* He wrote "The Story of Life Insurance" (1906) and "The Great American Fortunes and Their Making" (1907–1908) as well as articles on the railroads, the Sherman Anti-trust law, initiative and referendum in Oregon, Charles Evans Hughes in Albany, and another promising progressive governor in New Jersey named Woodrow Wilson.

George Kibbe Turner. Ex-newspaperman George Kibbe Turner replaced Steffens as *McClure's* urban expert. His chief themes were the corruption created by the political machines, the public service corporations, and the combination of the saloon, the liquor interests, vice, and crime. Turner, alone among the muckrakers, argued that the spread of the business ethic was the solution, not the cause of the trouble. Where Steffens had found the businessman at the root of municipal corruption, Turner believed that methods such as the city commission form of government which had rebuilt Galveston, Texas, after the hurricane of 1900, could save the cities. While Burton Hendrick blamed the businessmen for looting the New York City municipal utilities and relied on the Sherman Anti-trust law to regulate business, G. K. Turner was sure that enlightened capitalism could do what was necessary by itself. In a series on "The Masters of Capital in America" (1910–1911) written with trust expert John Moody, Turner argued that business itself, if it were big enough and free enough, could stabilize the economy. Hendrick and Turner, along with the western individualist and story-teller Alfred Henry Lewis who wrote on the world of the bosses, Tammany Hall, and the robber barons for *Human Life* and *Cosmopolitan*, and Will Irwin, *Collier's* expert on the city bosses and "The American Saloon," formed the conservative wing of the muckrake pack. They believed that the solutions to the problems on which they wrote would come from within the industrial system itself or from the individualistic, competitive nature of man.

There was a tendency after 1906 for the journalists to turn from political exposure to political commentary and reformist politics. Mark Sullivan, who had helped spark the patent medicine crusade began editing a regular column on national affairs in *Collier's*. Tariff reform, political in-fighting during the Taft Administration (1909–1913), the rise of congressional insurgency, and the return of ex-President Theodore Roosevelt to the political wars drew the journalistic interest into more accustomed channels.

Conservation. The muckrakers were to make one more big splash in national politics during 1909–1910. It was set against the background of the growing split in the Republican ranks between the conservatives and an insurgent group. The issue was conservation and the handling of natural resources, which along with regulation of the corporations had been a central concern for Theodore Roosevelt and his supporters.

Conservation was a complicated problem. The traditional American policy was to open up the national domain for private development as rapidly as possible. Much of the land and its wealth fell into the hands of large corporate interests. Nevertheless, the small developers, homesteaders, sheep and cattlemen, as well as the larger mining and lumber interests strongly favored continuation of the open policy. To most Westerners this was the traditional and proper course. The new Roosevelt approach was "preservation"— land management and planning, based upon national regulation and permanent government land holding. It ran counter to tradition and enterpriser economics, and perhaps even the statutory powers of the national government.

The Taft Administration. When William Howard Taft became President in 1909, he replaced Roosevelt's Interior Secretary with a western enterpriser named Richard Ballinger. Ballinger had been a reform mayor in Seattle and President Roosevelt had made him head of the General Land Office. While eliminating inefficiency and corruption in the Land Office, he had also come into conflict with Roosevelt's number one conservationist, Gifford Pinchot, the Chief Forester. Upon becoming Interior Secretary Ballinger opened up the public lands for sale and development, a policy bound to lead to trouble. President Taft himself explained the issue as "rather abstruse, but there are a great many people in favor of conservation no matter what it means."

The Fight over Alaskan Lands. A conflict erupted over a collection of claims to Alaskan coal lands. A speculator named Clarence Cunningham had applied for a number of claims on behalf of various clients and had arranged the sale of options on that land to a high finance syndicate composed of the Morgan and Guggenheim interests. A young Land Office investigator named Louis Glavis reported that the so-called "Cunningham Claims" appeared to be fraudulent and pressed for a prolonged investigation. Ballinger who was close to the claimants and had actually been their lawyer between his Washington stints, directed that the investigations be quickly completed and the claims validated. Finding no support within his own department, Glavis appealed to Gifford Pinchot who had remained as Chief Forester in the Agriculture Department.

Collier's and Hampton's. The public land issue was already heating up. *Collier's Weekly* and *Hampton's* applied the match. *Collier's* editor, Norman Hapgood, had criticized the sensationalistic writings of Tom Lawson's "Frenzied Finance" and David Graham Phillips' "The Treason of the Senate." Aided by the founder's son, Robert Collier, and Mark Sullivan, Hapgood built the magazine into a leading national influence. *Collier's* was on the way to a million copy circulation. Advertising man B. B. Hampton had taken over the "snappy story" *Broadway Magazine.* First with Theodore Dreiser and then himself as editor, he turned *Hampton's* into an impressive vehicle for good fiction and social criticism.

The Whitewashing of Ballinger. *McClure's* and *Hampton's* had already published articles on national resources problems when a *Collier's* editorial focused on the Secretary of the Interior. "Ballinger Should Go," it proclaimed. The controversy over water-power sites, Alaskan coal land entry, and the fight between Taft's Interior Secretary and Chief Forester Gifford Pinchot became a news sensation. When Land Office investigator Glavis was fired, *Collier's* printed his side of the story entitling it "The Whitewashing of Ballinger," (*see Reading No. 18*) and set Christopher P. Connolly to work on the affair. Connolly, who had been Prosecuting Attorney of Butte, Montana during the internecine struggles of the copper interests, was considered the leading journalistic authority on western problems. *McClure's* had published his narrative of the political wars in Montana, and *Collier's* used him to cover labor-management violence and to report on land swindles and railroad corruption in the West. At the same time, articles appeared in *Hampton's* by the water power authority, John L. Mathews. Together the two magazines opened up on the Taft Administration. Congress authorized an investigation, and Forester Pinchot lobbied against the Administration in Congress and forced a reluctant President Taft to fire him.

Collier's soon after received warning that the Administration planned to have the conservative Joint Congressional Investigating Committee (1911) exonerate Ballinger, after which a million dollar libel suit would be launched against *Collier's*. An emergency meeting was held at the house of Henry L. Stimson, later to be Herbert Hoover's Secretary of State and the World War II Secretary of War. The *Collier's*-Pinchot group selected the brilliant "people's lawyer" Louis D. Brandeis to represent Glavis before the Committee. Since *Collier's* was not officially a party to the conflict, the strategy was to concentrate on the defense of Glavis.

Presidential Creditability. The hearing was the sensation of the journals and the Washington social season, and Louis Brandeis made it positively explosive. Brandeis was struck by a sudden thought that Taft could not possibly have read all the evidence on which the President claimed to have made the decision to fire Glavis. Eventually the Administration was forced to admit that evidence had been held back from the Committee, that the "basis" of the President's decision had been written after Glavis was discharged and predated, and that the President's statement exonerating the Secretary of the Interior had been prepared under the direction of Ballinger himself.

Although a majority of the Committee dependably praised the Administration, the revelation of untruthfulness left the President's reputation damaged. *Collier's* was not sued. In the elections later that year, the Republican Party lost control of Congress for the first time since 1892, although the Republican progressives did well. Secretary of the Interior Richard Ballinger resigned in the spring of 1911. The Cunningham Claims were never granted. The split in the Republican Party and between Taft and Theodore Roosevelt widened.

CHAPTER 8

Society: Poverty, Children, Women, Labor, and the Blacks

Beyond the Middle Classes. Throughout its brief history, the central muckraker concern had been with big business; it was at the heart of the corruption and the politics about which they wrote. As the muckrake journalists evolved from being mere reporters to becoming social analysts, they began seeing more than their newspaper experience had trained them for. Many of them were dealing for the first time with classes, people, and problems unknown in their middle-class lives and values. The 1900s were exciting times, and the muckrakers were becoming particularly aware of what an industrial and urbanizing society meant. The popular magazines, run by editors such as S. S. McClure and Norman Hapgood, often drove their writers into new explorations. In a time of change, the journalists mingled with social and settlement workers, tenement house and court reformers, labor leaders, socialists, and social gospelers, as well as bosses, businessmen, and politicians.

After the successful insurance, meat, medicine, and railroad series of 1905–1906, the muckrakers came to explore industrial warfare, and to educate their readers about the conditions of working women, children, the poor and the slums. They dealt with the problems of the saloon and prostitution, the courts and the prisons, what it meant to be Oriental or black in America, and the economic ties and the social turmoils of the churches.

Poverty. In his book *From The Depths: The Discovery of Poverty in the United States* (1956), Robert Bremner points out that the dawning twentieth century was broadening its views. Instead of focusing on the pauper who could not support himself and became a

52

charge on society and the object of charity, attention was increasingly concentrated on the conditions that produced poverty and kept the working poor in a state of "insufficiency and insecurity." Society began to turn its gaze away from the alms house, the poor house, and the orphanage toward the tenement, the mine, the cotton mill, the laundry, and the packinghouse.

The Children. No picture in Upton Sinclair's *The Jungle* is more heart-wrenching than that of the child, Stanislovas, whose frostbitten ears and fingers had made him convulsively terrified of the snow, beginning to cry when cold weather comes again, and being beaten to make him venture out to his job at the lard machine. Sinclair used the sensation caused by *The Jungle* to write further about the "Children of Packingtown" in *Success*. Then to avoid the food preparation topic which had drawn attention away from his central labor-socialist message, Sinclair next wrote about the children in the glass-blowing industry, in a manuscript which no one would publish.

Edwin Markham and the Hoe-Man. The San Francisco school teacher Edwin Markham was greatly moved by the depiction of brutalizing toil in "The Angelus," a painting by the French painter, Jean François Millet. Markham wrote a poem about it and his description of the peasant, "bowed with the weight of centuries, he leans upon his hoe," became famous. Hearst's *Cosmopolitan* brought Markham to New York to write about children in the factories. His 1906–1907 series on "The Hoe-Man in the Making" (*see Reading No. 19*) used official governmental reports to show that life was more unbelievable than fiction. In *Children in Bondage* (1914) he reworked his material together with George Creel and Ben Lindsay to aid the growing national movement to ban child labor.

The Kid's Judge. Denver Municipal Judge Benjamin B. Lindsay found that his juvenile crime cases stemmed from poverty. His attempt as "the kid's judge" to deal with the causes led him into bitter conflict with the business and political worlds, and he became both subject and author for the magazines. Lincoln Steffens called him "The Just Judge" in *McClure's*, describing how Lindsay was attempting to stop "the machinery of justice" and pull children "out of its grinders" through his new "juvenile court." (*See Reading No. 20.*) Although *Everybody's* had to send a collaborator out to Denver to help him rewrite it, Judge Lindsay's autobiographical "The Beast and the Jungle" became another magazine link between public information and reform.

Women. Despite the success of Ida Tarbell's Standard Oil history, the magazines themselves were not above exploiting the working woman. Rheta Childe Dorr discovered this when *Everybody's* tried to deny her co-authorship of its account of her experiences as a working woman. However, *Hampton's* published her early liberationist articles, which balanced the more conventional accounts of the women's role and struggle which William Hard wrote for *Everybody's* and Ida Tarbell offered in the *American Magazine.* William Hard, Burton Hendrick, Charles Edward Russell, and others wrote on women and children in industry and the carnage of industrial accidents, prison brutalities and the convict lease system, prostitution, and the saloon. Marshalling their factual studies under titles such as "De Kid Wot Works at Night," "Making Steel and Killing Men," "Beating Men to Make Them Good," "A Burglar in the Making," and "Daughters of the Poor," they helped fuel the newly emerging concern for what was called the "less fortunate."

Labor. A number of social topics particularly interested the muckrakers: industrial warfare, vice and the saloon, race, the churches, and the press. The early twentieth century was the period of the greatest industrial violence in American history. Its most basic causes, as summed up retrospectively in 1969 by the National Violence Commission (Eisenhower Commission), were "employers' denial of the right of labor to organize and their attempt to break strikes." The journalists could hardly have avoided industrial conflict. Upton Sinclair had gone to Chicago to write about the packinghouse strike, and Ray Stannard Baker helped touch off the "exposure business" by his articles on the Pennsylvania coal fields. Those who wrote about labor sooner or later had to deal with industrial violence in the West, particularly the open warfare in the Colorado mining regions, the assassination of Idaho's ex-governor Frank Steunenberg (1905), and the bombing of the Los Angeles *Times* building (1911).

With the exception of Lincoln Steffens and the socialists, the journalists showed much middle-class conservatism. Although they had progressed beyond Ray Stannard Baker's initial emphasis on economic individualism ("The Right to Work"), Burton Hendrick, C. P. Connolly and others shared Roosevelt's antagonism toward unions and union leaders, particularly when violence was involved. Assuming a parity of strength between the corporations and the unions, they spoke out for the consumer "caught in the middle" between big business and the "labor trusts."

Industrial Lawlessness. As they investigated conditions in the West, most of them came to feel that the mining corporations were basically at fault. "Back of the lawlessness which has been attributed to the miners," the lawyer-journalist C. P. Connolly wrote, "was the greed and corruption of the capitalists" who controlled legislatures and the law, and "prodded men, ordinarily law-abiding, to anger and violence." However, the muckrakers were not totally one-sided in their support of labor. When union leaders Haywood, Moyer, and Pettibone were charged with ordering the Steunenberg slaying, G. K. Turner helped prepare the "Confessions" of the bombsetter Harry Orchard for publication in *McClure's*. *Collier's* C. P. Connolly lamented the flaws in the law through which the labor leaders were eventually freed, although he did not complain about the way in which the accused had been arrested in Colorado and secretly shipped to Idaho without a chance to resist extradition in the courts. In 1911, at the Los Angeles *Times* dynamiters' trial, Connolly continued his feud with the labor defense lawyer Clarence Darrow.

A number of journalists did identify with the working classes and their struggle, but they did not promote the issues as a major theme in their writings. Lincoln Steffens, who had become an admirer of the Socialist leader Eugene V. Debs, acted as a go-between for the defense of the *Times* dynamiters and the Los Angeles business community and tried to work out a vast social compromise. Steffens never joined the Socialist Party because he was too busy trying to turn big businessmen and city bosses into a kind of *herrenfolk* socialist leadership. Upton Sinclair came to muckraking as a socialist, while Charles Edward Russell joined the party in 1908. David Graham Phillips toyed with radicalism in his later novels. However, Upton Sinclair's *The Jungle* was the only work which concentrated on the problems of the working classes, and no full-fledged muckrake series was ever waged to reveal the plight and suffering of the working man.

The Saloon. Prostitution and the saloon were the particular concerns of the later, more conservative muckrakers, G. K. Turner and Will Irwin. Both problems were important to the progressives. As James Timberlake points out in *Prohibition and the Progressive Movement* (1963), prohibition linked the middle-class concern about the growing power of big business with the discontent of urban-industrial workers. The muckrakers saw most things through middle-class eyes. Prohibition was considered enlightened reform, sought by the middle classes to benefit the working classes and the poor.

The saloon keeper was often deeply involved with the brewers, the liquor interests, prostitution, and politics. In "The Shame of the Cities," Lincoln Steffens told of how someone had emptied the St. Louis municipal assembly by rushing in with the cry "Mister, your saloon is on fire." *McClure's* G. K. Turner identified cities "from scarlet Babylon to smoky Chicago," as "the great market place[s] of dissipation." Chicago, he wrote somewhat incorrectly, was the center of violent crime in America. As Turner saw it, the criminal saloonkeepers, gambling, prostitution, and dope were the chief causes of the crime. It was through the cooperation of the saloon, the ward boss, and the police official that crime and corruption (the "exploitation of savagery") in Chicago was organized. The liquor dealers, primarily the brewers, would stop at nothing to increase their profits. In a celebrated article on "The Daughters of the Poor" (1909), Turner detailed the organized seduction of young immigrant girls for the red light districts of American cities, linking white slavery and city politics. (*See Reading No. 21.*)

In his series on "The American Saloon" for *Collier's,* Will Irwin presented a similar picture of "the poor man's club" caught in the system of crime, vice, and corruption. He too saw the brewers as the chief offenders. In their drive for profits, they pushed the saloon-keeper outlets into breaking the laws. Irwin's article, "More About 'Nigger Gin,' " linking drinking and race seemed to rouse the most interest. In black bars throughout the South, a specially bottled "nigger gin" was sold. It was advertised and labeled with pictures of naked white women, playing upon the fears of the white, if not the fantasies of the black. Irwin maintained that in the South, the rising tide of prohibition was seen as a means of controlling the black underman. However, Irwin's article reflected only a superficial image of American race relations.

Following the Color Line. Ray Stannard Baker's "Following the Color Line" series (1906–1908) was one of the most important achievements of magazine journalism. In 1906 Baker went South to describe how "the ocean of antagonism between the white and Negro races" had produced a "savage" riot against the black people of Atlanta. The cause was superficially simple: the Negro disliked the poor white and the poor white hated the Negro. "It is in these lower strata of society, where the races rub together in unclean streets," Baker wrote, "that the fire is generated." It was in the "swarming saloons and dives" of Decatur and Peters Streets in Atlanta that trouble errupted. However, the problems were more widespread. "How would you feel," Baker was asked, "if you saw a governor, a mayor, a sheriff, whom you could not oppose at the polls, encourage by deed or word or both, a mob of 'best' and worst citizens to slaughter your people in the streets and in their own homes and in their places of business?" This had been the experience of black Atlanta.

The response to his race riot stories in *McClure's* was so favorable that Baker continued to research and write on the subject for the next two years. The result was a comprehensive survey of the conditions and life of the American Negro, which Gunnar Myrdal praised and used in his classic *An American Dilemma* (1944) a third of a century later.

Once started, Baker traveled in the Black Belt and in large cities and small towns of both the North and South, interviewing and corresponding with racial leaders. Although the national magazines carried many articles about Southern racism and racial problems, Baker was not prepared for the savagery of the race riot and lynch mob. Nor was he prepared for the Southern preoccupation with race. In one of his early articles he told of a young Negro who worked in the home of a prominent Atlanta family. One day his family asked what the white people talked about at the dinner table. "The boy thought for a moment; then he said: 'Mostly they discusses us culled folks.' "

With his characteristic "fact pictures," Baker showed that racial feeling, segregation, and violence were a growing national ill. Although by his final article in 1908 Baker had softened his position as he ended his flirtation with the Socialist Party, he saw economic competition along with racial repulsion at the root of the trouble. He argued that the restlessness of the blacks, "An Ostracized Race in Ferment," was part of a world-wide awakening of the "underman" who would not "keep his place." In a private exchange of letters President Roosevelt maintained that slavery (and by implication, discrimination) ran contrary to the American ethical values. Baker argued back that the fight against slavery and racial discrimination came from their being undemocratic.

Baker has been fairly criticized for his stereotyping, his backing off from immediate change, and for favoring Booker T. Washington's accommodationism over W. E. B. Du Bois' demands for equality. Nevertheless, like the other muckrakers he rejected biological views of inequality or criminality, and he offered extensive testimony of what would today be called the "institutional racism" of American life. (*See Reading No. 22.*)

The Spiritual Unrest. By 1908, Baker had finished "Following the Color Line" and had moved away from the socialists. He was vexed by the loss of a railroad law suit, and increasingly involved in local politics in East Lansing, Michigan. Apparently the success of his extremely popular stories of rural contentment, published under the pseudonym of "David Grayson" did not satisfy his quest for community spirit. In his notebooks, where he tried out his ideas, he wrote "How I am driven back again & again upon Jesus Christ."

Whether the David Grayson stories and religion were a personal escape or a social solution is not clear. Whichever it was, organized religion offered little help. In a chaotic but widely read *American* series on "The Spiritual Unrest," Baker found that the churches mirrored the problems of society. They reflected the growing class divisions of a materially prosperous society which too often lacked a concern for the children, the poor, the immigrant, and the Negro. The churches, at least from a social standpoint, didn't seem very Christian. It was not just the slum landlordism of New York's Trinity Church which both Baker and Charles Edward Russell (*see Reading No. 23*) flayed. Baker maintained that in their ministrations to the wealthy, the churches had lost their spiritual leadership and no longer had any message for the common people. Along with the "new Christianity" of the social gospel theologian Walter Rauschenbusch, many of those who were "unchurched" but socially committed seemed to show the proper faith. There was a highly religious quality, he wrote, about believing in the abolition of poverty.

Neither Baker nor any of the other muckrakers offered a prescription for such a new twentieth-century abolitionist crusade. Generally speaking, the beginnings of the welfare state were overshadowed by the struggle for the regulation of business, and the journalists wrote about social problems as basically the products of an unrestrained economic system. Men thought in terms of scarcity, not abundance. They did not talk about doing away with poverty. This would have meant a radical view of social possibilities which transcended the experience and the society they knew, and the muckrakers—and the progressives—were not radicals. They did not think in terms of a radical solution to poverty or to economic, racial, or sexual exploitation. Nor did the muckrakers have a vision of the modern bureaucratic welfare society. Their journals nowhere launched sustained campaigns for regulation of wages, hours, and working conditions for women and children, for the prohibition of child labor, for unemployment and accident insurance, for guarantees of jobs, housing, medical care, and for decent standards of living, education, and recreation. In some ways, their social ideas were still those of the village, not the modern, complex society. However, in what the poverty-historian Robert Bremner calls "a factual generation," concern was stirring, and the journalists graphically helped raise the level of public awareness.

CHAPTER 9

The State of the Press

Most of the muckrakers were professional journalists. As newspapermen in New York and Chicago, they reported and edited for publishers such as William Randolph Hearst and Joseph Pulitzer before moving on to the magazines. They were the best there was. As professionals they were very conscious of the role of the press and how it was performing. Despite many a fighting editor and many a notable crusade, the muckraker evaluation of the press was not very favorable. Will Irwin, Samuel Hopkins Adams, Ray Stannard Baker, Charles Edward Russell, and Mark Sullivan wrote on such topics as "What's Wrong with the A.P.?" "Tainted News Methods of the Liquor Interests," "Religious Journalism and the Great American Fraud," "How the Railroads Make Public Opinion," "How Business Controls the News," "The Associated Press and Calumet," "The Patent Medicine Conspiracy Against the Freedom of the Press." They had hard things to say about the newspapers, and a decade later Upton Sinclair in *The Brass Check* (1919) extended the condemnation to many of the muckrake journals which were willing to print an exposé, as long as it didn't go "too far."

Self-censorship. Will Irwin's series on "The American Newspaper" for *Collier's* in 1911 was the most thorough study of the press. In his autobiography, Irwin later reflected on how he had arrived at the idea for the series. "In cities where gangs of machine politicians were stealing the shingles off City Hall, often local newspapers kept silence until some magazine writer like Lincoln Steffens came from outside to unsheathe his rake." Why? Often a paper was the strictly private enterprise of its publisher, who put in what he wished and kept quiet about corporate greed, special privilege, and other publishers' libel suits. In other cases advertisers and big business used pressure to keep "harmful" news out of the papers. The end product of such censorship, Irwin summed up, was boss rule and the protection of bad social conditions.

Amid stories of great editors and the rise of battling newspapers, Irwin told how the Chicago papers described the "white slave traffic," but passed over the department store whose low wage scales drove its girl employees into the brothels. The press skipped over the stories of how the brewers herded newspapers into line against prohibition, how Standard Oil greased its way to press approval, and how advertisers and editors hushed up a bubonic plague outbreak in San Francisco. (*See Reading No. 24.*)

Even when a newspaper was not "owned" or deliberately dishonest, its position was difficult. "Capital is timid," Irwin explained; "Journalism should be brave." However, it faced an anomalous quandry. "Upstairs, journalists, willing to risk life itself that they may 'get the story,' to hazard friendship and personal esteem that they may attack special privilege and vested injustice— for such is the spirit and custom of the craft. Downstairs—usually— a publisher frightened at the loss of a hundred dollars in advertising."

The Muckrake Journals. What happened to the muck-rake? Nine journals enlisted in the ranks during the great campaigns between 1903 and 1912: *McClure's, Everybody's* (and its short-lived companion *Ridgway's*) *Collier's Weekly, Cosmopolitan, American Magazine, Human Life, Hampton's, Success,* and *Pearson's.* After resigning from *Collier's* in a fight over whether the magazine would endorse Theodore Roosevelt or Woodrow Wilson in 1912, Norman Hapgood had a late go at muckraking in *Harper's Weekly.* With its campaign against the patent medicines, *The Ladies Home Journal* briefly joined company, and the *Woman's Home Companion* struck out at the "slavery" of child labor. B. O. Flower's *Arena* and Lyman Abbott's *Outlook* lent political support. Walter Hines Page's *World's Work* darted in and out of the movement, and when William Randolph Hearst bought *World To-Day* and changed its name to *Hearst's Magazine,* he gave it a belated muckrake run.

The Death of the Muckrake. By 1912, the year that Theodore Roosevelt and Woodrow Wilson locked horns for the presidency, muckraking was dying. Historians and radicals have argued over whether the magazines were killed by the "interests" and the advertisers, or whether muckraking used up its welcome and its audience. Running a national journal was a big business proposition. It cost a great deal of money to be a cheap magazine. The owners engaged in speculative schemes, bought expensive presses and printing plants, and took risks on new book publishing companies. Sudden increases in circulation were costly if advertising rates could not increase proportionately, but failure to grow in circulation meant that income could not keep up with operations. The magazines needed large profits and ample bank financing. It is possible that there was just not a sufficient market to support the numerous ventures that the initial muckrake success brought into the field. Harold Wilson, the later historian of *McClure's Magazine and the Muckrakers* (1970) concludes that "mounting costs drove the magazines to the wall."

The Hand of Big Business? It could hardly be expected that big business liked muckraking. Charles Edward Russell, for instance, claimed that his beef trust series caused the withdrawal of meat, soap, fertilizer, and railroad ads from *Everybody's*. It is likely that it was the editorial policies rather than the financial condition of *Success* and *Hampton's* that led the banks to refuse them operating cash. S. S. McClure and Robert Collier were forced to bring in monied partners. The *American* was purchased by the Crowell Publishing Company, which was related to the Thomas Lamont–J. P. Morgan interests, which the muckrakers had particularly pilloried. In the case of *Collier's*, P. F.'s son Robert lacked the financial skill of his founder-father and eventually the bankers and business managers took over. *Collier's* too eventually became a Crowell property.

Sometimes the business side of the magazine—"Downstairs," as Will Irwin called it—was cautiously fearful of offending advertisers. On other occasions, the new controlling interests deliberately soft-peddled muckraking. Ray Stannard Baker believed that this had happened on the *American*, and he, Ida Tarbell, and others resigned in 1915.

No Longer a Paying Proposition. Perhaps the handwriting on the wall was popular rather than financial. The various reforms of the Roosevelt era and Woodrow Wilson's "New Freedom" may have satisfied the middle-class clamor for control of business. A decade of muckraking may have jaded the popular taste. Frank Luther Mott, the leading student of American magazines, believed that the readers were tired of "shrill-voiced criticism." Perhaps there were just more journals than the field could support and it damaged them all. *Cosmopolitan*, *Collier's*, *McClure's* and the *American Magazine* switched to romance, achievement, more serialized fiction, pretty girls, and the short story. As *Everybody's* owner Erman J. Ridgway announced, muckraking was no longer a paying proposition.

No More Magazines for Everybody. In *Magazines in the Twentieth Century* (1964) Theodore Peterson perceptively points out that the successful nineteenth-century magazines were highbrows and not interested in reaching a mass market by satisfying mass tastes. The popular magazines which gave birth and platforms to muckraking were "magazines for everybody." They specialized in social criticism but had a well rounded offering of fiction, features, and illustrations as well. With the demise of muckraking, the popular magazines turned away from reform. Social criticism gravitated into the hands of what Peterson calls "the magazines of cultural minorities" such as the *Nation* and the *New Republic*, with a limited, specially interested clientele. Occasionally the mass public journals have taken the muckrake route, but only during the first decade of the twentieth century were the muckrake journals "magazines for everybody."

CHAPTER 10

Conclusions

Moral Indignation and Facts. What is the significance of the muckrakers? What did they do and how much did it matter? The historian Alexander B. Callow, Jr., in writing about New York City's Tweed Ring (1859–1871) scandals, stated that the essential elements for a crusade against civic corruption are "moral indignation and facts." The muckrakers supplied both and projected them on a national level. The muckrake trademark was the detailed factual story, complete with names, dates, documents, and mind-staggering tally sheets about the extent and cost of the corruption. The journalists shuttled in and out of New York City to write on municipal elections in St. Louis, land frauds in the Pacific Northwest, bosses in Cincinnati, capital-labor strife in Pennsylvania and Idaho, vice and corruption in Chicago (their favorite municipal target), rebates in the oil fields, and manipulation on Wall Street.

Ward bosses protected crime and prostitution. Aldermen and mayors sold franchises and stole from city treasuries. Legislatures did the same things on the state level, and sent businessmen to the United States Senate to do the same thing nationally. Land frauds, mineral frauds, timber frauds, water frauds, tariff frauds, and stock frauds abounded. Not only were favors bought and the government corrupted at all levels, but the public was cheated and squeezed, labor was exploited, consumers poisoned, investors swindled, companies looted, and poverty perpetuated. This was the muckrake picture of a twentieth-century urban and capitalist America. (*See Reading No. 25.*)

National Lawlessness. The muckraking journalists performed an important role. First, they made the American middle class conscious of corruption. Second, they linked together all of the different kinds of wrong-doing into a broad picture of the malfunction of

American society. Third, they offered an explanation for it all. The effective cause of the national corruption was the concentration of vast economic power. They had many names for it: the Corporations, High Finance, Frenzied Finance, the Trusts, the System, the Interests, Plutocracy, and Monopoly. Although the new economic giants were the instruments of national wrong-doing, the basic fault lay in the values and institutions of society. The laws and moral codes of a more placid agrarian system did not hold for a major urban and industrial society.

Before the end of the second decade of the twentieth century, a majority of Americans would live in towns and cities, an increasing number in the great exploding metropolises. Urban America needed more than the profit motive, the trolley car, and the ward boss to guide it. The prime collective achievement of the muckrakers was to point out the conflict between the growth of large scale private economic power and the needs of the new national American society.

The term the muckrakers used for this conflict was "lawlessness," but they used it in such a way as to cause confusion. Sometimes it meant felonious assault and crime in the streets, sometimes industrial warfare, sometimes institutional malfunction, sometimes the behind-the-scenes "invisible government" of the political and economic bosses, and sometimes the aggressions of capital. The muckrakers were no more successful than anyone else in working out the degree to which the criminal codes governing the behavior of individuals could be made to apply to the behavior of large economic organizations.

Middle-class Optimism. Otis Graham, Jr., who has studied the biographies of several hundred progressives, sums up the muckrakers by saying that most of them merely tried to warn the middle class that "its food was adulterated, its insurance funds misused, its stocks watered, and its government full of graft." If this were all they did, then the muckrakers would rank as important forerunners of the still infant field of consumer protection. Consumerism, however, was only a part of their concern.

The muckrakers represented a principle much discounted today by political realists, radicals, and conservatives alike. Like most progressives, the journalists did not see society as divided and subdivided into a multitude of interest groups, primarily economically based. Many subsequent commentators have pointed out that this was their weakness, but perhaps it was also their strength. Basically optimistic, they believed that democracy and progress went hand-in-hand. The people were good. With information and guidance, the people would be capable of selecting proper principles and leaders. Accumulating wealth and the materialistic standards which Ida Tarbell summed up with the phrase "commercial machiavellianism" could be overcome through public opinion, altruism, a return to moral standards, and the regeneration of political and economic leadership. Society could escape from its lawlessness, or anarchic, materialistic disorganization, and regain proper moral solidarity.

Lincoln Steffens sought to convince tycoons and bosses that running a city for the benefit of its people was more exciting than running a railroad for profit. He called it "practical Christianity," and probably most of the muckrakers would have accepted such a term to describe their goal. Excepting only Tom Lawson ("Frenzied Finance"), they were serious about their efforts to do good for America. When the press referred to them as crusaders, it fitted their own self-image.

Privilege as Treason. The most frequent criticism of the journalists is that they saw the world as divided between good and bad men, and that they offered little more than the old political cry of "throw the rascals out." This is the common textbook image. The fact that the journalists focused their stories on the industrialist, the railroad magnate, the banker, the senator, and the political boss was misleading. Most of the muckrakers didn't much care whether the Democrats or the Republicans were in office. Both parties were much alike, and party was a device to mislead the public, not inform or represent it.

Nor was the "business government" a solution for any of the muckrakers, except G. K. Turner. Businessmen in government constituted much of the problem. The lure of special privilege was too strong for them. As Lincoln Steffens recalled explaining it to the elite Jonathan Club in San Francisco, special privilege was the prize which society gave for evil-doing. "Let's take down the offer of a reward," he had said. "Let's abolish—privileges." In reply to an Episcopal Bishop who asked where it all began, Steffens went on, "You want to fix the fault at the start of things. Maybe we can. Most people, you know, say it was Adam. But Adam, you remember, he said it was Eve, the woman; she did it. And Eve said no, no, it wasn't she; it was the serpent. And that's where you clergy have stuck ever since. You blame the serpent, Satan. Now I come and I am trying to show you that it was, it is, the apple." *

The muckrake ethic developed into a demand for a new political morality in an age of organization. The men in power acted "treasonably," to use David Graham Phillips' and Lincoln Steffens' term, when they squeezed their great fortunes out of the tenement dwellers, subway riders, farmers, shippers, small businessmen, investors, oil producers, workers, and consumers.

Education. The muckrake instrument for the creation of the national morality was education. "Facts, facts, and more facts," were the way to reform. That path did not lead back to American individualism, which a majority of the muckrakers soon left behind, but to an awakened leadership and public. As "reform" Darwinists, they believed that public concern and enlightened public interest leadership could produce the proper environment for a better society. The great William James, at Harvard, perceived the role which the journalists had taken as social educators. The leadership of American thought, he commented, was shifting from the universities to the ten-cent magazines.

Acceptance of an Enterpriser Society. The muckrakers agreed that the problem was one of monopoly, greed, and institutional failure. They differed on how to solve it. At one end of the spectrum, there were those who believed that individualism, competition, or business government was the answer. For the majority of the journalists, whether they believed in competition or bigness, the proper instrument for change was the regulatory state. During the progressive period, that state began to emerge. Today, the United States is a system of regulatory capitalism, mixed with some natural resource socialism, Keynesian or indirect business cycle controls, occasional crisis-time direct controls on wages and prices, and corporate, state, and national welfarism. Still the nation has remained an enterpriser society, with the key production decisions in the hands of the businessmen, somewhat circumscribed and prodded by government. Although they did not foresee the other developments, the muckrakers saw the necessity of basic components of regulation and private enterprise. Only a few, G. K. Turner

* From *The Autobiography of Lincoln Steffens*, Vol. II (New York: Harcourt Brace Jovanovich, Inc., 1958), p. 574.

and A. H. Lewis on the Right, and Upton Sinclair, Gustavus Myers, Charles Edward Russell—and perhaps Lincoln Steffens—on the Left, believed that the economy could do without either the government or the enterpriser-businessman.

Muckraker Politics. In a very real way, the journalists shared an uneasy partnership with Theodore Roosevelt. Most of them were originally enthusiastic about the President, but came to cringe under his attack and to doubt his sincerity. He, in turn, refused to share the middle of the road with anyone else. He feared that the muckrakers were not politically "realistic" and were stirring up a popular discontent that might take a dangerously socialistic direction. Actually, the muckrakers helped prepare public support for the President's regulatory solutions and softened up the political opposition. They collaborated on the major progressive era achievements: the Pure Food and Drug Act (1906), the Meat Inspection Act (1906), the Hepburn Act (1906) strengthening the Interstate Commerce Commission, and conservation. They helped bring about New York State's regulation of the insurance industry, and the Seventeenth Amendment to the national Constitution for the direct election of senators.

In an electoral republic, the attack which the popular journals waged against "corrupt" public officials whom the muckrakers identified as "friends of the interests" was an important political factor. On the plus side, Tom Johnson was reelected Mayor of Cleveland; Joseph Folk went to the state house in Missouri; Robert M. La Follette became a United States Senator, and Nelson W. Aldrich, "the representative of all the interests," retired from the Senate. Joseph T. Hadley in Kansas and Theodore Roosevelt would probably have filed anti-trust suits against Standard Oil without Ida Tarbell's articles. The muckrakers did not dream up the income tax amendment, tariff reform, or Woodrow Wilson's Clayton and Federal Trade Commission Acts. Probably as many of Lincoln Steffens' municipal reformers were defeated as got elected, and despite G. K. Turner's grand jury testimony, prostitutes still walked the streets of American cities. On the whole, the muckrakers were more the supporters of reform laws and publicizers of the results of grand jury investigations than the originators.

For a decade, the magazine journalists were dramatic spokesmen on popular issues and probably second only to President Theodore Roosevelt in reaching a national audience. Democratic governments are dependent on two-way communication between the people and their government. Periodic elections need continual supplementation. In most cases there is no way to measure the impact of public opinion on the governmental process. Presidents, legislators, and bureaucrats follow it when they find it convenient, ignore it when they feel they can or must, and usually rationalize their actions, even to themselves. At the same time, particularly in the public life of a democratic society, the values of men in power and the tasks they set for themselves and their societies are often touched by popular attitudes and demands. Between 1902 and 1912, the muckrakers had a prominent role in such a shaping.

The Public Interest. Historians give the muckrakers credit for helping father the modern, middle-class, regulatory state, but there is growing question over whether they should be praised for it. Modern critics tend toward two critical conclusions. They assert that regulatory capitalism is run by and for the capitalists. "Public morality" and "the public interest" are decried as meaningless guidelines which conceal the nature of interest and power in society. The middle classes pass off their own comfortable place within society as universal morality. "Public morality" is their morality, and "the public interest" is their interest. Political realists such as George Mowry and Richard Hofstadter have described the muckrakers and their fellow progressives as members of the old, Protestant, middle-class leadership, which reacted to the loss of status, prestige, and power to the big corporations and an organizational society.

Neither the muckraker-socialists nor the muckraker-enterprisers understood the nature of bureaucracy and modern government. It is questionable whether they did much better with the nature of groups and interests. Interests and groups conflict; the muckrakers thought in terms of order. They were rationalists. Their middle-class backgrounds and "practical idealism" dulled their awareness of the nature of power. Seeing the havoc which unrestrained economic power was creating in society, their solution was an ethical one. They assumed that there was basically one public rather than many, and therefore they believed that everyone could be educated to the acceptance of a single "public interest" as a guide. This would do away with private or group use of power. They did not recognize the pluralistic or interest-group society which A. F. Bentley wrote about in his pioneering *The Process of Government* (1908) or that Charles

Beard was describing to his government classes at Columbia University. Basically the appeal of both liberals and socialists was that men should rise above group, faction, and greed. While the conservative muckrakers saw interest and greed as healthy individualistic forces, the muckraker-progressives believed that national regulation and the public interest would lift society above corporate and group selfishness. The muckraker-socialists looked to collective ownership to perform the same feat. None recognized the highly heterogeneous nature of American society.

The Muckrakers and the Middle Classes. More than half of the magazine journalists had been recruited from the big city newspapers. They often wrote about the problems of labor, the immigrant, the black, the Oriental, the women who worked in the sweatshops and the children who tended the looms, and the tenements and the poor. They called for social and welfare reforms, as well as regulation of the railroads and an end to municipal corruption. Social reform had to come from the public-spirited citizenry. By progressive standards this meant their own, old stock, white, middle-class America. Somewhat fearful of the masses, the muckrakers did not consider sharing power with labor and the other underclasses or groups in society.

Though less followers of John Locke's absolute defense of property and less committed to individual economic enterprise than they have been accused of being, most of the muckrakers were liberals. On the crucial "liberal" values, they believed in the people and in change, were not distrustful of government, and were reservedly critical of private property. The people were good and would be trustworthy when informed. Great changes had already taken place, and more were necessary. There was a tendency to believe that reform and major changes came periodically, rather than continuously. Abolitionism and the Civil War were one such wave. Another, they believed, was cresting. As the other Roosevelt, FDR, would phrase it a quarter of a century later, they believed that their own generation had that "rendezvous with destiny." They tended to see the conflict of property vs. individual rights in consumer, wage, and small property terms. The governmental role was primarily that of a regulatory agent in the economy.

The muckrakers did not like concentrated wealth or misbehaving trusts, but they rejected a return to a Jeffersonian world of small-scale individual enterprisers. Most wanted a regulatory capitalism, but even the muckraker-socialists did not glimpse either the possibilities or the dangers of big government.

Muckraker Socialism. Upton Sinclair used the royalties from *The Jungle* to build a communitarian colony on the palisades of the Hudson River, which he called Helicon Home Colony. In *The Industrial Republic* (1907) he described this experiment in group living. Drawing together the various socialist doctrines of alienation, corporate concentration, the surplus, and the capitalist breakdown, Sinclair hoped for a world based on the community of interest of the workers, not on increasing production. Once 'the output was no longer set by profit-dictated maldistribution, there would be enough for everyone. While his path toward this cooperative society was no more clear than today's communitarianism, Sinclair alone among the muckrakers sought this form of radical transformation of the capitalist society. It was because he believed in such a goal that he had become a muckraker in the first place.

Only Charles Edward Russell and Gustavus Myers found that their muckraking carried them all the way into the socialist camp. Lincoln Steffens hovered vaguely around socialism, more interested in the public-spirited use of power, than doing away with power. Charles Edward Russell had been an Iowa Greenbacker, a single-taxer, and an early foe of the railroads. His experience with a capitalist society that produced the slums, prisons, and poverty, led him to working-class sympathies and an analysis based upon surplus production. Much more than Upton Sinclair's brand, Charles Edward Russell's radicalism was typical of the American brand of eclectic socialism.

Making Regulation Work. The basic problems of regulatory capitalism are how to regulate and toward what ends. The attention of muckrakers, historians, and the general public has usually focused on the battle to get legislatures and congresses to pass laws. The anti-trust suit against Standard Oil, the struggles for the Pure Food and Drug law, the Hepburn Act, and the Federal Trade Commission were dramatic. The press and history books concentrate on the passing of such bills but do not usually examine what happens afterwards. Neither the Sherman and Clayton Anti-trust laws nor the regulatory system have prevented the growth or misbehavior of concentrated economic and political power.

Although United States Senators seldom go to jail, judges, congressmen, legislators, and former governors are from time to time likely to. Processors adulterate and corporations pollute. Standard Oil was dissolved by the Supreme Court in 1911 and is today the largest industrial corporation in the world, and five oil companies, not one, head the list of American giant corporations. Prisons deprave rather than correct, and the inmates of the Arkansas penitentiary probably would not have been much worse off if the state had started to lease them out again. Safety laws are not enforced in the mines. Undereducated and undernourished children may be out of the factories, but they still work in the migratory stream or languish in the ghettos of the inner cities. Once the principle of regulation is accepted and an agency created and empowered to regulate, the problems have really just begun. The question has always been more complicated than simply a choice between private profit and public interest. The public interest is complex, multiple, and contradictory.

The corporate firm and industry employ and produce. Their financial health is a vital part of "the public interest." Historians who decry the failure of the muckrakers to offer objective or working standards for regulatory capitalism have been just as unable to provide them. However, the critic does not have to accept the radical view that business created the regulatory state as its own instrument, to agree that business and inertia have captured and held most state and national regulatory agencies.

The regulatory state is staffed by individuals from those industries that it is supposed to supervise. Governors and presidents have failed to appoint effective public interest representatives. The political system, the voters, and the media have failed to demand legislators and regulators who will combine a concern for the public interest with the long range, healthy development of industry. The impartial expert, anchored within the protected civil service strata of the regulatory agency and government, has often turned out to be a timid and routineering bureaucrat. Legislative failure to fund properly has often been as deadly as economic interest and political pressure. Judicial paths have often been as slow as bureaucratic ones, and the complexities of the American legal system have often made the political problems seem simple by comparison. The regulatory system has never shown any signs of being an automatic mechanism. It needs a great deal of pressure from outside to get and keep it going, and it usually has received the wrong kind. The consumer's champion of the 1960s and 1970s, Ralph Nader, has pointed out that he is unlike the earlier muckrakers because they had no follow up. He intends to be different.

The Need for Carry Through. Probably what regulatory capitalism needs most is to develop and institutionalize public-interest pressure and follow-through. The error of the muckrakers was the belief that government—the regulator—itself could produce this follow-through. The regulatory experience clearly indicates that sufficiently financed and mandated structures, such as consumer counsels and representatives, are needed. So is continuous pressure from outside, representing the public or general interest, as well as more narrowly directed labor and farmer interest groups. Such pressures must be focused on the political parties as well as on the regulatory agencies. Consumer leagues and cooperatives, lobbies and public interest law firms, unions, study groups, and "raiders" need the spur, support, and platform that the muckrakers and the media of their day, the popular magazines, provided in initiating the system of regulatory capitalism in the first place.

The Muckrake Contribution. The great contribution of the muckrakers was that they developed a new form of detailed, factual, investigatory journalism which exposed the problems and confusion of the American social system at the beginning of the twentieth century. The existence of the need was indicated, as young Walter Lippmann pointed out, by the remarkable interest with which the American middle-class public read the muckrake writing. The journalists and Theodore Roosevelt helped lead the silent middle classes into progressivism. The main resources of the journalists were honest indignation, the facts, and the belief that there was some sort of essential value in society which could be called "the public interest." If they were naïve to believe that a public interest existed, more sophisticated modern critics are also naïve if they believe that either communitarian withdrawal or the power competitions of different "interest" groups alone can handle society's problems and directions.

The muckrakers focused their attack on giant capitalism without, for the most part, being willing to seek an alternative to the capitalist system. They looked to regulation without an understanding of the nature and difficulties of big government, or regulation itself. They sought to help the underclasses without a sufficient awareness that they were themselves a class. They did not realize that an important part of the solution to the problems of the underclasses lay in sharing the possession of power, not just in the conscience of governments and the overclasses.

The problems, limitations, and failures in defining what the public interest is stands at the core of their failure to remake society. But without a continuous reawakened and fueled concern for some value called "the public interest"—however it is defined, and however much it changes—any modern society is in peril.

The Pulitzer prize-winning historian, Richard Hofstadter, wrote in his book on *The Progressive Historians* (1968), that what the muckraking journalists and the popular novelists were getting at was a picture of what their society was actually like. "Reality" was "the inside story." It was "the bribe, the rebate, the bought franchise, the sale of adulterated food, the desperate pursuit of life in the slums." Such "reality" was not to be found "in the standard textbooks on constitutional law, political science, ethics, economics, or history." It was to be found, Hofstadter wrote, in the writing of Henry Demarest Lloyd, the novelists Frank Norris and Theodore Dreiser, and in Upton Sinclair's *The Jungle*, David Graham Phillips' *Susan Lennox*, Ida Tarbell's *The History of Standard Oil*, and Lincoln Steffens' *The Shame of the Cities*.*

* Richard Hofstadter, *The Progressive Historians* (New York: Alfred A. Knopf, Inc., 1968), p. 184.

Part II

Readings

Cartoon Views of Financial
Capitalism and Monopoly Power*

Political cartooning is older than the history of the Republic. In 1754, Benjamin Franklin helped produce a widely circulated picture of a snake, divided into thirteen pieces, entitled "JOIN OR DIE." Caricatures in the colonial newspapers pilloried George III and his ministers for all the ills which caused the Revolution.

Influenced by the French political satirist Honoré Daumier (1808–1870) and Thomas Nast (1840–1902) of Harper's Weekly, *illustrated social criticism became a highly developed art in America. Nast's slashing attacks in the 1870s upset New York's corruptionist "Boss" Tweed who complained that although his followers couldn't read, they couldn't help seeing "them damned pictures." Nast created the political symbols of the Republican elephant, the Democratic donkey, and the Tammany tiger. His successors found many others in Uncle Sam, Columbia, the Yankee farmer, the Southern colonel, and the Westerner with a broad brimmed hat.*

Charles Dana Gibson, James Montgomery Flagg, and Howard Chandler Christy's drawings of pretty girls made the heart of every American male beat a little faster. The humor magazines Life, Judge, *and* Puck, *copying England's* Punch, *produced an explosion of caricature and criticism. Joseph Keppler depicted plutocratic moneybag senators, Frederick B. Opper drew the trust giants, and Homer Davenport covered Mark Hanna's suit with dollar signs. By the 1890s the comic strip and political cartoon were part of the daily newspapers.*

---

* J. P. Morgan cartoon reprinted from the N.Y. *World* in *Everybody's*, 23 (September, 1910), p. 297. John D. Rockefeller, Sr. reprinted from William Jennings Bryan's *The Commoner* in *The Literary Digest*, XXX (May 6, 1905), p. 654.

Banner headlines, screaming magazine covers, beckoning advertisements, dramatic photographs, and slashing political cartoons became accustomed magazine fare and an important part of the muckrake attack. As one of the best, W. A. Rogers commented, "After all, we cartoonists are merely reporters with a drawing-pen or brush instead of a pencil."

Two of the most famous cartoons were C. R. Macauley's image of the banker J. P. Morgan and Spencer's caricature of John D. Rockefeller. The picture of Morgan, seated on his throne, holding the reins of economic power in the United States, was reprinted in Everybody's for Lincoln Steffens' series on the "money power." When John D. Rockefeller, Jr. compared Standard Oil to the American Beauty Rose which could be produced in all its splendor "only by sacrificing the early buds that grew up around it," Spencer showed John D. Rockefeller, Sr. pruning his garden.

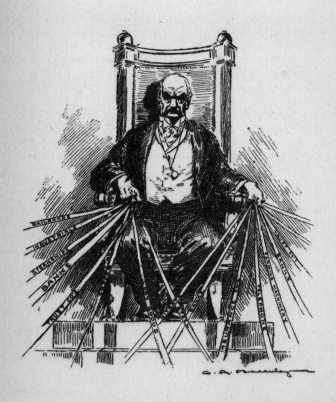

READING NO. 2

Muckrake Beginnings:
McClure's Editorial*

In an editorial at the back of the January, 1903 issue of his magazine, S. S. McClure pointed out the connection between the three lead articles on

* *McClure's*, XX (January, 1903), p. 336.

*current social and economic problems. Lincoln Steffens' article on how the
mayor and his police chief brother ran corruption in Minneapolis featured
reproductions of the grafters' ledger book. Ida M. Tarbell told about John
D. Rockefeller's attempt to control the Pennsylvania oil fields, and Ray
Stannard Baker reported on the life of miners who refused to support a
strike in the coal-fields. In his editorial, McClure maintained that together
the three articles constituted "an arraignment of American character."
Corruption was becoming the national pattern. With this editorial, the
muckrake movement was born, although it was not until three years later
that Theodore Roosevelt would give it its name.*

CONCERNING THREE ARTICLES IN THIS NUMBER
OF MCCLURE'S, AND A   COINCIDENCE THAT
MAY SET US THINKING

How many of those who have read through this number of the
magazine noticed that it contains three articles on one subject? We did
not plan it so; it is a coincidence that the January MC CLURE'S is such
an arraignment of American character as should make every one of us
stop and think. How many noticed that?

The leading article, "The Shame of Minneapolis," might have been
called "The American Contempt of Law." That title could well have
served for the current chapter of Miss Tarbell's History of Standard Oil.
And it would have fitted perfectly Mr. Baker's "The Right to Work." All
together, these articles come pretty near showing how universal is this
dangerous trait of ours. Miss Tarbell has our capitalists conspiring
among themselves, deliberately, shrewdly, upon legal advice, to break
the law so far as it restrained them, and to misuse it to restrain others
who were in their way. Mr. Baker shows labor, the ancient enemy of
capital, and the chief complainant of the trusts' unlawful acts itself
committing and excusing crimes. And in "The Shame of Minneapolis"
we see the administration of a city employing criminals to commit
crimes for the profit of the elected officials, while the citizens—Americans of good stock and more than average culture, and honest, healthy
Scandinavians—stood by complacent and not alarmed.

Capitalists, workingmen, politicians, citizens—all breaking the law, or
letting it be broken. Who is left to uphold it? The lawyers? Some of the
best lawyers in this country are hired, not to go into court to defend
cases, but to advise corporations and business firms how they can get
around the law without too great a risk of punishment. The judges? Too
many of them so respect the laws that for some "error" or quibble they
restore to office and liberty men convicted on evidence overwhelmingly

McClure's Magazine

VOL. XX   *JANUARY, 1903*   NO. 3

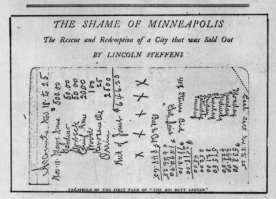

THE SHAME OF MINNEAPOLIS

The Rescue and Redemption of a City that was Sold Out

BY LINCOLN STEFFENS

FAC-SIMILE OF THE FIRST PAGE OF "THE BIG MITT LEDGER"

THE OIL WAR OF 1872

BY IDA M. TARBELL

Author of "The Life of Lincoln"

CHAPTER III OF THE HISTORY OF THE STANDARD OIL COMPANY

THE RIGHT TO WORK

The Story of the Non-striking Miners

BY RAY STANNARD BAKER

convincing to common sense. The churches? We know of one, an ancient and wealthy establishment, which had to be compelled by a Tammany hold-over health officer to put its tenements in sanitary condition. The colleges? They do not understand.

There is no one left; none but all of us. Capital is learning (with indignation at labor's unlawful acts) that its rival's contempt of law is a menace to property. Labor has shrieked the belief that the illegal power of capital is a menace to the worker. These two are drawing together. Last November when a strike was threatened by the yard-men on all the railroads centering in Chicago, the men got together and settled by raising wages, and raising freight rates too. They made the public pay. We all are doing our worst and making the public pay. The public is the people. We forget that we all are the people; that while each of us in his group can shove off on the rest the bill of to-day, the debt is only postponed; the rest are passing it on back to us. We have to pay in the end, every one of us. And in the end the sum total of the debt will be our liberty.

READING NO. 3

Lincoln Steffens and The Shame
of the Cities*

Between October, 1902 and November, 1903, McClure's featured articles by Lincoln Steffens on corruption in St. Louis, Minneapolis, Pittsburgh, Philadelphia, Chicago, and New York. The last of his series aimed at helping the re-election of Seth Low's reform administration in New York. However, the Tammany machine won, and the next month, December, 1903, Steffens attempted to sum up the reasons why "good government" was having so much trouble in America. His explanation appeared as the introduction to his collected articles, The Shame of the Cities, which McClure's published in 1904.

When I set out on my travels, an honest New Yorker told me honestly that I would find that the Irish, the Catholic Irish, were at the bottom of it all everywhere. The first city I went to was St. Louis, a German city. The next was Minneapolis, a Scandinavian city, with a leadership of New Englanders. Then came Pittsburg, Scotch Presbyterian, and that was what my New York friend was. "Ah, but they are all foreign populations," I heard. The next city was Philadelphia, the purest American community of all, and the most hopeless. And after that came Chicago and New York, both mongrel-bred, but the one a triumph of reform, the other the best example of good government that I had seen. The "foreign element" excuse is one of the hypocritical lies that save us from the clear sight of ourselves.

Another such conceit of our egotism is that which deplores our politics and lauds our business. This is the wail of the typical American citizen. Now, the typical American citizen is the business man. The typical business man is a bad citizen; he is busy. If he is a "big business man" and very busy, he does not neglect, he is busy with politics, oh,

*Lincoln Steffens, *The Shame of the Cities* (New York, 1904), pp. 2–6.

very busy and very businesslike. I found him buying boodlers in St. Louis, defending grafters in Minneapolis, originating corruption in Pittsburg, sharing with bosses in Philadelphia, deploring reform in Chicago, and beating good government with corruption funds in New York. He is a self-righteous fraud, this big business man. He is the chief source of corruption, and it were a boon if he would neglect politics. But he is not the business man that neglects politics; that worthy is the good citizen, the typical business man. He too is busy, he is the one that has no use and therefore no time for politics. When his neglect has permitted bad government to go so far that he can be stirred to action, he is unhappy, and he looks around for a cure that shall be quick, so that he may hurry back to the shop. Naturally, too, when he talks politics, he talks shop. His patent remedy is quack; it is business.

"Give us a business man," he says ("like me," he means). "Let him introduce business methods into politics and government; then I shall be left alone to attend to my business."

There is hardly an office from United States Senator down to Alderman in any part of the country to which the business man has not been elected; yet politics remains corrupt, government pretty bad, and the selfish citizen has to hold himself in readiness like the old volunteer firemen to rush forth at any hour, in any weather, to prevent the fire; and he goes out sometimes and he puts out the fire (after the damage is done) and he goes back to the shop sighing for the business man in politics. The business man has failed in politics as he has in citizenship. Why?

Because politics is business. That's what's the matter with it. That's what's the matter with everything,—art, literature, religion, journalism, law, medicine,—they're all business, and all—as you see them. Make politics a sport, as they do in England, or a profession, as they do in Germany, and we'll have—well, something else than we have now,—if we want it, which is another question. But don't try to reform politics with the banker, the lawyer, and the dry-goods merchant, for these are business men and there are two great hindrances to their achievement of reform: one is that they are different from, but no better than, the politicians; the other is that politics is not "their line." There are exceptions both ways. Many politicians have gone out into business and done well (Tammany ex-mayors, and nearly all the old bosses of Philadelphia are prominent financiers in their cities), and business men have gone into politics and done well (Mark Hanna, for example). They haven't reformed their adopted trades, however, though they have sometimes sharpened them most pointedly. The politician is a business man with a specialty. When a business man of some other line learns the business of politics, he is a politician, and there is not much reform left in him. Consider the United States Senate, and believe me. . . .

But there is hope, not alone despair, in the commercialism of our politics. If our political leaders are to be always a lot of political merchants, they will supply any demand we may create. All we have to do is to establish a steady demand for good government. The bosses have us split up into parties. To him parties are nothing but means to his corrupt ends. He "bolts" his party, but we must not; the bribe-giver changes his party, from one election to another, from one county to another, from one city to another, but the honest voter must not. Why? Because if the honest voter cared no more for his party than the politician and the grafter, then the honest vote would govern, and that would be bad—for graft. It is idiotic, this devotion to a machine that is used to take our sovereignty from us. If we would leave parties to the politicians, and would vote not for the party, not even for men, but for the city, and the State, and the nation, we should rule parties, and cities, and States, and nation. If we would vote in mass on the more promising ticket, or, if the two are equally bad, would throw out the party that is in, and wait till the next election and then throw out the other party that is in—then, I say, the commercial politician would feel a demand for good government and he would supply it. That process would take a generation or more to complete, for the politicians now really do not know what good government is. But it has taken as long to develop bad government, and the politicians know what that is. If it would not "go," they would offer something else and, if the demand were steady, they, being so commercial, would "deliver the goods."

But do the people want good government? Tammany says they don't. Are the people honest? Are the people better than Tammany? Are they better than the merchant and the politician? Isn't our corrupt government, after all representative?

READING NO. 4

The Corruption of the States*

Lincoln Steffens soon found that most of the cities' problems reached into state government, and perhaps even beyond. In 1904–1905 he wrote studies

* Lincoln Steffens, "Enemies of the Republic," *McClure's*, XXII (April, 1904), p. 587.

*of corruption and reform in Missouri, Illinois, Wisconsin, Rhode Island,
Ohio, and New Jersey. In 1906,* McClure's *gathered his articles in book
form under the title of* The Struggle for Self-Government. *In his first
article on Missouri, he maintained that "big business" was "the source and
the sustenance" of America's bad government.*

ENEMIES OF THE REPUBLIC

The Political Leaders Who Are Selling Out The
State Of Missouri, And The Leading Business
Men Who Are Buying It—Business As
Treason—Corruption As Revolution

Every time I attempted to trace to its sources the political corruption
of a city ring, the stream of pollution branched off in the most
unexpected directions and spread out in a network of veins and arteries
so complex that hardly any part of the body politic seemed clear of it. It
flowed out of the majority party into the minority; out of politics into
vice and crime; out of business into politics, and back into business;
from the boss, down through the police to the prostitute, and up through
the practice of law, into the courts; and big throbbing arteries ran out
through the country over the State to the Nation—and back. No wonder
cities can't get municipal reform! No wonder Minneapolis, having
cleaned out its police ring of vice grafters, now discovers boodle in the
council! No wonder Chicago, with council-reform and boodle beaten,
finds itself a Minneapolis of police and administrative graft! No wonder
Pittsburg, when it broke out of its local ring, fell, amazed, into a State
ring! No wonder New York, with good government, votes itself back
into Tammany Hall!

They are on the wrong track; we are, all of us, on the wrong track.
You can't reform a city by reforming part of it. You can't reform a city
alone. You can't reform politics alone. And as for corruption and the
understanding thereof, we cannot run 'round and 'round in municipal
rings and understand ring corruption; it isn't a ring thing. We cannot
remain in one city, or ten, and comprehend municipal corruption; it isn't
a local thing. We cannot "stick to a party," and follow party corruption;
it isn't a partizan thing. And I have found that I cannot confine myself to
politics and grasp all the ramifications of political corruption; it isn't
political corruption. It's corruption. The corruption of our American
politics is our American corruption, political, but financial and indus-

trial too. Miss Tarbell is showing it in the trust, Mr. Baker in the labor union, and my gropings into the misgovernment of cities have drawn me everywhere, but, always, always out of politics into business, and out of the cities into the state. Business started the corruption of politics in Pittsburg; upholds it in Philadelphia; boomed with it in Chicago and withered with its reform; and in New York, business financed the return of Tammany Hall. Here, then, is our guide out of the labyrinth. Not the political ring, but big business,—that is the crux of the situation. Our political corruption is a system, a regularly established custom of the country, by which our political leaders are hired, by bribery, by the license to loot, and by quiet moral support, to conduct the government of city, state, and nation, not for the common good, but for the special interests of private business. Not the politician, then, not the bribe-taker, but the bribe-giver, the man we are so proud of, our successful business man—he is the source and the sustenance of our bad govern-ment.

READING NO. 5

The History of the Standard
Oil Company*

Ida Tarbell's History *ran in* McClure's Magazine *in eighteen install-ments from November, 1902 through October, 1904. It was the most carefully researched and probably the most famous and best piece of work produced by the muckrakers. The third installment in January, 1903, along with articles by Lincoln Steffens and Ray Stannard Baker, produced S. S. McClure's editorial "discovery" of the movement. Although she gathered her material with diligence and attempted to present it fully and fairly, there was no concealing her affection for the independent producers of the oil regions and her belief that the rise of the Standard Oil Company was a great misfortune.*

* Ida Tarbell, "The History of the Standard Oil Company." I, McClure's, XX (November, 1902), p. 16. II, McClure's, XX (January, 1903), pp. 259–260.

I

Indeed, by the opening of 1872, life in the Oil Regions had ceased to be a mere makeshift. Comfort and orderliness, even opportunities for education and for social life, were within reach. It was a conquest to be proud of, quite as proud of as they were of the fact that their business had been developed until it had never been, on the whole, in so satisfactory a condition.

Nobody realized more fully what had been accomplished in the Oil Regions than the oil men themselves. Nobody rehearsed their achievements so loudly. "In ten years," they were fond of saying, "we have built this business up from nothing to a net product of six millions of barrels per annum. We have invented and devised all the apparatus, the appliances, the forms needed for a new industry. We use a capital of $200,000,000, and support a population of 60,000 people. To keep up our supply we drill 100 new wells per month, at an average cost of $6,000 each. We are fourth in the exports of the United States. We have developed a foreign market, including every civilized country on the globe."

But what had been done was, in their judgment, only a beginning. Life ran swift and ruddy and joyous in these men. They were still young, most of them under forty, and they looked forward with all the eagerness of the young who have just learned their powers, to years of struggle and development. They would solve all these perplexing problems of over-production, of railroad discrimination, of speculation. They would meet their own needs. They would bring the oil refining to the region where it belonged. They would make their towns the most beautiful in the world. There was nothing too good for them, nothing they did not hope and dare.

Suddenly, at the very heyday of this confidence, a big hand reached out from nobody knew where, to steal their conquest and throttle their future. The suddenness and the blackness of the assault on their business stirred to the bottom their manhood and their sense of fair play, and the whole region arose in a revolt which is scarcely paralleled in the commercial history of the United States.

II
MR. ROCKEFELLER BEGINS ALL OVER AGAIN

If Mr. Rockefeller had been an ordinary man the outburst of popular contempt and suspicion which suddenly poured on his head would have thwarted and crushed him. But he was no ordinary man. He had the powerful imagination to see what might be done with the oil business if it could be centered in his hands—the intelligence to analyze the problem into its elements and to find the key to control. He had the essential element to all great achievement, a steadfastness to a purpose once conceived which nothing can crush. The Oil Regions might rage, call him a conspirator and those who sold him oil traitors; the railroads might withdraw their contracts and the legislature annul his charter; undisturbed and unresting he kept at his great purpose. Even if his nature had not been such as to forbid him to abandon an enterprise in which he saw promise of vast profits, even if he had not had a mind which, stopped by a wall, burrows under or creeps around, he would nevertheless have been forced to desperate efforts to save his business. He had increased his refining capacity in Cleveland to 10,000 barrels on the strength of the South Improvement Company contracts. These contracts were annulled, and in their place was one signed by officials of all the oil-shipping roads refusing rebates to everybody. His geographical position was such that it cost him under these new contracts 50 cents more to get oil from the wells to New York than it did his rivals on the Creek. What could he do?

Mr. Rockefeller Gets a Rebate

He got a rebate. In spite of the binding nature of the contracts signed in New York on March 25th by representatives of all the railroads, before the middle of April the Standard Oil Company was shipping oil eastward from Cleveland for $1.25—this by the sworn testimony of Mr. H. M. Flagler before a commission of the Ohio State Legislature, in March, 1879. How much less a rate than $1.25 Mr. Rockefeller had before the end of April the writer does not know. Of course the rate was secret, and he probably understood now, as he had not two months before, how essential it was that he keep it secret. His task was more difficult now, for he had an enemy active, clamorous, contemptuous, whose suspicions had reached that acute point where they could believe nothing but evil of him—the producers and independents of the Oil Regions. It was utterly impossible that he should ever silence this enemy, for their points of view were diametrically opposed.

They believed in independent effort—every man for himself and fair play for all. They wanted competition, loved open fight. They considered that all business should be done openly—that the railways were bound as public carriers to give equal rates—that any combination which favored one firm or one locality at the expense of another was unjust and illegal.

Mr. Rockefeller's Opinions and Character

Mr. Rockefeller's point of view was different. He believed that the "good of all" was in a combination which would control the business as the South Improvement Company proposed to control it. Such a combination would end at once all the abuses the business suffered. As rebates and special rates were essential to this control, he favored them. Of course Mr. Rockefeller knew that the railroad was a public carrier, and that its charter forbade discrimination. But he knew that the railroads did not pretend to obey the laws governing them, that they regularly granted special rates and rebates to those who had large amounts of freight. That is, you could bargain with the railroads as you could with a man carrying on a strictly private business depending in no way on a public franchise. Moreover, Mr. Rockefeller knew that if he did not get rebates somebody else would; that they were for the wariest, the shrewdest, the most persistent. If somebody was to get rebates, why not he? This point of view was no uncommon one. Many men held it and felt a sort of scorn, as practical men always do for theorists, when it was contended that the shipper was as wrong in taking rates as the railroads in granting them.

Thus, on one hand there was an exaggerated sense of personal independence, on the other a firm belief in combination; on one hand a determination to root out the vicious system of rebates practised by the railway on the other a determination to keep it alive and profit by it. Those theories which the body of oil men held as vital and fundamental Mr. Rockefeller and his associates either did not comprehend or were deaf to. This lack of comprehension by many men of what seems to other men to be the most obvious principles of justice is not rare. Many men who are widely known as good, share it. Mr. Rockefeller was "good." There was no more faithful Baptist in Cleveland than he. Every enterprise of that church he had supported liberally from his youth. He gave to its poor. He visited its sick. He wept with its suffering. Moreover, he gave unostentatiously to many outside charities of whose worthiness he was satisfied. He was simple and frugal in his habits. He never went to the theater, never drank wine. He was a devoted husband, and he gave much time to the training of his children, seeking to develop in them his own habits of economy and of charity. Yet he was willing to strain every nerve to obtain for himself special and illegal privileges from the railroads which were bound to ruin every man in the oil business not sharing them with him. Religious emotion and sentiments of charity, propriety and self-denial seem to have taken the place in him of notions of justice and regard for the rights of others.

Unhampered, then, by any ethical consideration, undismayed by the clamor of the Oil Regions, believing firmly as ever that relief for the disorders in the oil business lay in combining and controlling the entire refining interest, this man of vast patience and foresight took up his work. The day after the newspapers of the Oil Regions printed the report of the Congressional Committee on Commerce denouncing the South Improvement Company as "one of the most gigantic and dangerous conspiracies ever attempted," and declaring that if it had not been checked in time it "would have resulted in the absorption and arbitrary control of trade in all the great interests of the country."

READING NO. 6

Ida Tarbell and the Rockefeller Image*

In her History, Ida Tarbell focused on John D. Rockefeller as the malignant force behind the growth of the Standard Oil monopoly. Afterwards she wrote three additional articles indicting him as a victim of a "money-passion" and a major cause of the "commercial machiavellianism" which she believed was ruining American society. The Image which she created of the elder Rockefeller has lasted to the present day.

These then are the tactics which for thirty-five years John D. Rockefeller has been applying to business. Is it strange that he has grown richer and richer as the years went by until to-day he is called the richest man in the world? How rich he is nobody knows—perhaps he does not know himself. Twelve years ago, in 1892, when the Standard Oil Trust was dissolved, Mr. Rockefeller owned certificates for 256,854 shares of the stock, between one-fourth and one-third of the entire trust. His dividends on this amount were in that year over three million; in 1896 nearly eight million; in 1900 over twelve million. . . . And his Standard Oil stock is only one of his dividend earners. Mr. Rockefeller's personal property in Cleveland, Ohio, outside of Standard Oil interests

* Illustration from *The Literary Digest*, XXX (June 24, 1905), p. 949. Reading from Ida Tarbell, "John D. Rockefeller, A Character Study, I," *McClure's*, XXV (July, 1905), p. 249.

amounts probably to $10,000,000, and includes mortgages from $200 up to $500,000, real estate from remote city lots to his beautiful Forest Hill park of over 400 acres, beside stocks and bonds of all sorts.

Mr. Rockefeller has not squandered his income. He has applied it for thirty-five years to accumulating not only oil property but real estate—railroad stock, iron mines, copper mines, anything and everything which could be bought cheap by temporary depressing and made to yield rich by his able management. For thirty-five years he has worked for special privileges giving him advantages over competitors, for thirty-five years he has patiently laid net-works around property he wanted, until he had it surely corralled and could seize it; for thirty-five years he has depreciated values when necessary to get his prey. And to-day he still is busy. In almost every great financial manoeuvre in the country is felt his

supple, smooth hand with its grip of steel, and while he directs that which is big, nothing is too small for him to grasp.

Why does he do it? What does he want an income of $25,000,000 and more for? Not to spend like some splendid old Venetian in palaces and galleries, for none of the glories of the fine old-world life are known to him. Not to squander in riot. So far as the world knows, he is poor in his pleasures. Not to give away—his charities and bequests are small compared to his wealth. For what then? Why this relentless, cruel, insistent accumulation of money when you are already buried in it. There seems to be only one explanation, that Mr. Rockefeller is the victim of a money-passion which blinds him to every other consideration in life, which is stronger than his sense of justice, his humanity, his affections, his joy in life, which is the one tyrannous, insatiable force of his being. "Money-mad, money-mad! Sane in every other way, but money-mad," was the late Senator Hanna's comment on John D. Rockefeller. And the late Senator Hanna could not be accused of holding money in light regard.

READING NO. 7

In Defense of John D. Rockefeller*

The prize-winning historian Allan Nevins has written the best, and probably the definitive, biography of John D. Rockefeller. In it he praised Ida Tarbell's History *as "the most spectacular success of the muckraking school of journalism, and its most enduring achievement." At the same time, he complained that she "underrated" the constructive elements of the organizational revolution in American industry.*

While the Industrial Commission hearings were still fresh in public memory, the gifted Ida M. Tarbell published in *McClure's Magazine* the first installment of her *History of the Standard Oil Company* (November, 1902). The time, the magazine, and the writer combined to make this

* Allan Nevins, *Study in Power, John D. Rockefeller, Industrialist and Philanthropist*, Vol. II (New York: Charles Scribner's Sons, 1953), pp. 339–343.

serialized book the most spectacular success of the muckraking school of journalism, and its most enduring achievement. Theodore Roosevelt had now been in power for a year; he had begun his trust-busting by ordering a suit against the Morgan-Hill-Harriman creation, the Northern Securities Company; and his annual message in December called for new weapons against industrial monopoly. S. S. McClure and John S. Phillips had given their monthly a circulation and prestige such as no magazine of equal solidity and literary quality had ever enjoyed. Directly or indirectly, it reached nearly the whole literate public of America. As for Miss Tarbell, she was a daughter of the Oil Regions, where her father had been a prominent if unprosperous producer. Growing up amid the tumult and shouting of the wars between Producers' Association men and Standard men, the girl felt a fervent sympathy for the independents. A graduate of Allegheny College, a staff member first of the *Chautauquan* and then of *McClure's*, the author of brilliantly successful articles and of a path-breaking book on Lincoln, she had achieved by 1901 a well-earned reputation as a writer. Now she rose to her greatest opportunity.

Into her work on the Standard she threw all her industry, earnestness, and skill. She went through the mountainous testimony of the various investigations and law-suits; she searched the press; she traveled back to the Regions to interview people. When H. H. Rogers sent word through Mark Twain that he would talk with her, she held a number of conferences with him at 26 Broadway. Rogers's ostensible motive was to help make the story fair and complete, but he also wished to protect himself. Still other members of the Standard organization, with the approval of the directors, assisted Miss Tarbell with information until they became convinced that she had no intention of doing the combination justice. Then her facilities were cut off. In every respect but one her labors were as searching as four years' of toil and ample expense funds could make them. The principal deficiency of her work was that she sought out comparatively few of the hundreds of veterans of the oil industry, both supporters and opponents of the Standard, whom she might have seen. Historians must always regret that she did not make a wider search for evidence, and deal less frequently in half truths.

Although readers today are likely to find her sober, factual history difficult to read, in 1902–04 the public had a background of knowledge which lent the articles a stirring interest. Men now forgotten were then vivid public figures; legal battles now dimmed by time were then excitingly real. Before McClure, Phillips published the two volumes in 1904 it had made a deep impression on the public mind; the deeper because Miss Tarbell avoided the hysterical emotion of Lloyd and strove to document every part of her story. In book form the 550 pages of text, though containing few footnotes, were buttressed by 240 pages of appended source material. The gravamen of her indictment was simple. Rockefeller and his associates, she argued, had built up a combination which was admirable in its organized efficiency and power; but nearly every step in the construction of this vast industrial machine had been attended by fraud, coercion, or special privilege, which had debased the whole standard of American business morality.

Her book was received with an explosion of applause from press, pulpit, and political leaders. The only important dissenting voices came from certain economic reviews and from the *Nation*, which attacked the work as sensational, ignorant, and deliberately unfair. Indeed, taken as a whole, and with due allowance for the facts that Miss Tarbell wrote frankly as an *ex parte* representative of the Regions and had a faulty grasp of economic evidence, it merited the praise it received. It was the best piece of business history that America had yet produced. It collected an immense mass of data, arranged it clearly, and cast it into a pattern which most subsequent writers have followed. Reissued in 1925, the work stands beside Lincoln Steffens's *The Shame of the Cities*, John Spargo's *The Bitter Cry of the Children*, and Ray Stannard Baker's *Following the Color Line* as an enduring product of the early progressive movement.

Yet though the chapters on the pipe lines, the anti-trust suits, prices, marketing ("Cutting to Kill"), and "The Legitimate Greatness of the Standard" remain valuable to any student, some parts of the work took untenable ground. Miss Tarbell accepted Lloyd's fable of a prosperous oil industry in 1872 thrown into confusion and depression by the South Improvement plan, though in fact the industry was then depressed and chaotic. She credited the invention of the South Improvement scheme to Rockefeller and his associates, although it actually originated with the railroads. She blamed the collapse of the early efforts of the Regions men to organize upon Rockefeller's machinations, when the cause lay chiefly in their own bickering and greed. She treated rebating as the special sin of the Standard, not as an almost universal practice, with her much-praised independents as eager to get rebates as anybody. She failed to grasp the fact that quasi-autonomous branches of the Standard like Waters Pierce and Chess, Carley committeed their worst acts in defiance (as Carley admitted) of Standard authority. Giving Rockefeller an excessive prominence throughout, she never realized that Flagler was chiefly responsible for railway rate arrangements, or that Daniel O'Day's outrageous drawback of 1885 on George Rice's Marietta oil ("This peculiar development of the rebate system seems to have belonged exclusively to Mr. Rockefeller," wrote Miss Tarbell) was made without Rockefeller's knowledge. That is, she never comprehended that the

Standard was a federation rather than a despotism. And her book was open to a more basic indictment. She but dimly realized that American industry was undergoing an irresistible revolution—that the whole economic scene was being transformed. Inevitably, she exaggerated the destructive, and underrated the constructive, elements in this revolution.

READING NO. 8

Thomas W. Lawson and Frenzied Finance*

When the Wall Street manipulators squeezed out Tom Lawson, he revenged himself by "telling all" in a confused but spectacular exposé in Everybody's Magazine *in 1904–1905. The most important results were a heightened alarm about the growth of a "Money Power" in America and an investigation of the life insurance industry.*

Amalgamated Copper was begotten in 1898, born in 1899, and in the first five years of its existence plundered the public to the extent of over one hundred millions of dollars.

It was a creature of that incubator of trust and corporation frauds, the State of New Jersey, and it was organized ostensibly to mine, manufacture, buy, sell, and deal in copper, one of the staples, the necessities, of civilization.

It is a corporation with $155,000,000 capital, 1,550,000 shares of the par value of $100 each.

Its entire stock was sold to the public at an average of $115 per share ($100 to $130), and in 1903 the price had declined to $33 per share.

From its inception it was known as a "Standard Oil" creature, because its birthplace was the National City Bank of New York (the "Standard Oil" bank), and its parents the leading "Standard Oil" lights, Henry H. Rogers, William Rockefeller, and James Stillman.

It has from its birth to present writing been responsible for more hell than any other trust or financial thing since the world began. Because of it the people have sustained incalculable losses and have suffered untold miseries.

---

* Reprinted in Thomas W. Lawson, *Frenzied Finance, The Story of Amalgamated* (New York, 1905), pp. 1–5.

But for the existence of the National City Bank of New York, the tremendous losses and necessarily corresponding profits could not have been made.

I laid out the plans upon which Amalgamated was constructed, and, had they been followed, there would have been reared a great financial edifice, immensely profitable, permanently prosperous, one of the world's big institutions.

The conditions of which Amalgamated was the consequence had their birth in Bay State Gas. To explain them I must go back a few years.

In 1894 J. Edward Addicks, of Delaware, Everywhere, and Nowhere, the Boston Gas King, invaded the gas preserves of the "Standard Oil" in Brooklyn, N. Y., and the "Standard Oil," to compel him to withdraw, moved on his preempted gas domains in Boston, Mass.

Late in 1894 a fierce battle was raging in Boston between Gas King Addicks and Gas King Rogers; the very air was filled with denunciation and defiance—bribery and municipal corruption; and King Addicks was defeated all along the line and in full retreat, with his ammunition down to the last few rounds.

Early in 1895 I took command of the Addicks forces against "Standard Oil."

By the middle of 1895 the Addicks troopers had the "Standard Oil" invaders "on the run."

In August, 1895, Henry H. Rogers and myself came together for the first time, at his house in New York, and we practically settled the Boston gas war.

Early in 1896 we actually settled the gas war, and "Standard Oil" transferred all its Boston gas properties ($6,000,000) to the Addicks crowd.

In October, 1896, the whole Bay State Gas outfit passed from the control of Addicks and his cohorts into the hands of a receiver, and as a result of this receivership, with its accumulated complications, "Standard Oil," in November, 1896, regained all its old Boston companies, and in addition all the Addicks companies, with the exception of the Bay State Gas Company of Delaware.

In 1896 I perfected and formulated the plans for "Coppers," a broad and comprehensive project, having for its basis the buying and consolidating of all the best-producing copper properties in Europe and America, and the educating of the world up to their great merits as safe and profitable investments.

In 1897 I laid these plans before "Standard Oil."

In 1898 "Standard Oil" was so far educated up to my plans on "Coppers" as to accept them.

In 1899 Amalgamated, intended to be the second or third section of

"Coppers," was suddenly shifted by "Standard Oil" into the first section, and with a full head of steam ran out of the "City Bank" station, carrying the largest and best train-load of passengers ever sent to destruction on any financial trunk-line.

In 1899, after the allotment of the Amalgamated public subscription, the public for the first time, in a dazed and benumbed way, realized it had been "taken in" on this subscription, and a shiver went down America's financial spinal column.

In 1900, after the price of Amalgamated had slumped to 75 instead of advancing to 150, to 200, as had been promised, the "Standard Oil"-Amalgamated-City Bank fraternity called Wall Street's king of manipulators, James R. Keene, to the rescue, and under his adroit handling of the stock in the market Amalgamated was sent soaring over its flotation price of 100.

In 1901 Boston & Montana and Butte & Boston, after long delay, drew out of the "Standard Oil" station as the second section of Amalgamated, carrying an immense load of investors and speculators to what was at that time confidently believed would be Dollar Utopia; and the price of the enlarged Amalgamated fairly flew to 130. These were the stocks which I had originally advertised would be part of the first section of the consolidated "Coppers," and which, after Amalgamated had been run in ahead of them, I advertised would follow in due course.

In the latter part of 1901 President McKinley was assassinated, and the great panic which might have ensued was averted by the marvellous power of J. Pierpont Morgan.

Then the Amalgamated dividend, without warning and in open defiance of the absolute pledges of its creators, was cut, and the public, including even James R. Keene, found itself on that wild toboggan whirl which landed it battered and sore, at the foot of a financial precipice.

This, briefly, is the tortuous course of Amalgamated, and it is along this twisting, winding, up-alley-and-down-lane way I must ask my readers to travel if they would know the story as it is.

At the lower end of the greatest thoroughfare in the greatest city of the New World is a huge structure of plain gray-stone. Solid as a prison, towering as a steeple, its cold and forbidding façade seems to rebuke the heedless levity of the passing crowd, and frown on the frivolity of the stray sunbeams which in the late afternoon play around its impassive cornices. Men point to its stern portals, glance quickly up at the rows of unwinking windows, nudge each other, and hurry onward, as the Spaniards used to do when going by the offices of the Inquisition. The building is No. 26 Broadway.

26 Broadway, New York City, is the home of the Standard Oil. Its countless miles of railroads may zigzag in and out of every State and city

in America, and its never-ending twistings of snaky pipe-lines burrow into all parts of the North American continent which are lubricated by nature; its mines may be in the West, its manufactories in the East, its colleges in the South, and its churches in the North; its head-quarters may be in the centre of the universe and its branches on every shore washed by the ocean; its untold millions may levy tribute wherever the voice of man is heard, but its home is the tall stone building in old New York, which under the name "26 Broadway" has become almost as well known wherever dollars are juggled as is "Standard Oil."

READING NO. 9

Lawson and Life Insurance*

In writing about the "System" Thomas Lawson happened to mention the connection between Wall Street and the great life insurance companies, Mutual, Equitable, and New York Life. Public interest soon made this a major focus of his exposé. Eventually there was an investigation of the insurance companies, which made the counsel Charles Evans Hughes famous and led to more stringent laws regulating the industry.

When I began to write "Frenzied Finance" I specifically stated that I should not concern myself with men, but with principles. I held that to put an end to the plundering of the people required more than the denunciation of individual criminals; that the real peril lay in the financial device through which the plundering was done and the "machine" developed for their operation. The "machine" is the tremendous correlation of financial institutions and forces that I call the "System," and the most potent factor in the "System" is the life insurance combine—the three great insurance companies, the New York Life, Mutual Life, and Equitable, with their billion of assets and the brimming stream of gold flowing daily into their coffers. That I should have to discuss the relation between the "System" and these great institutions was inevitable. . . .

* Reprinted in Thomas W. Lawson, *Frenzied Finance, The Story of Amalgamated* (New York, 1905), pp. 419, 421–422.

I was recently waited upon by an important man.

"Lawson, what are you doing in life insurance?" he asked.

"Giving facts about the life-insurance branch of a 'System' which is foully plundering the people," I answered.

"What are you trying to do?"

"Educate the millions of life-insurance policy-holders to their present peril; after they are educated, arouse them to quick, radical action."

"What are you going to do?" he asked.

"I am going to cause a life-insurance blaze that will make the life-insurance policy-holders' world so light that every scoundrel with a mask, dark-lantern, and suspicious-looking bag will stand out so clearly that he cannot escape the consequences of his past deeds, nor commit new ones."

"Have you figured the consequences to yourself?"

"Having no interest in what the consequences may be to myself in performing what I have decided is a sacred duty, I have not."

READING NO. 10

Burton J. Hendrick and the Heart of the Life Insurance Problem*

Tom Lawson generated the excitement, but it remained for Burton J. Hendrick to explain clearly and soberly what had really happened to the life insurance industry. This he did in a seven part series in McClure's *in 1906.*

I

THE SURPLUS: THE BASIS OF CORRUPTION

For the last thirty-five years a constant warfare has waged in the United States between the good and the bad in life insurance. On one side have ranged honesty, economy, and fair and liberal treatment of the

---

* I. Burton J. Hendrick, "The Story of Life Insurance," *McClure's* XXVII (May, 1906), pp. 36–37; II. XXVIII (November, 1906), pp. 61–62.

insured; on the other, dishonesty, extravagance, and absolute disregard of policy-holders' rights. Certain companies have treated life insurance as a great beneficient institution, organized for the purpose of protecting the weak and the dependent against adverse fortune; others have regarded it largely as a convenient contrivance for enriching the few men who happened to have usurped control.

In this thirty-five years the history of American life insurance has been one of progressive degeneration. The people have forgotten the old ideals; have persistently abandoned good life insurance and taken up with bad. They have for the larger part ignored the teachings of our great American leaders—men like Elizur Wright, of Massachusetts, the originator of nearly everything that is best in the American system; Jacob L. Greene, of Hartford; and Amzi Dodd, of New Jersey, and have sought the leadership of men who have degraded the whole institution. They have thus displaced the United States from the world leadership in life insurance which it formerly held, and have made what was one of our greatest claims to national distinction the cause of what is, in many ways, our most shameful national scandal.

To show this deterioration in quality we need not necessarily look far. The most popular companies, indeed, have largely ceased to do a life insurance business at all. If you study the literature they circulate, you will find the life insurance feature of their contracts only incidentally mentioned. They talk little about protection of one's family, but much about savings banks, investments, guaranteed incomes, five per cent Consols, and gold bonds. They ask you to buy their policies not that thereby you may provide financial protection for your dependents, but that you may thereby reap financial advantage yourself. They appeal, not to your sense of responsibility, but to your cupidity. They preach life insurance not as a boon to the poor and the defenceless, but to the fortunate and the rich. In a word they have grafted upon the simple life insurance idea endless investment and gambling schemes, most of which are fallacies and some of which are palpable frauds. Consequently hundreds of thousands profit little, or not at all, from the insurance feature of their contracts. In the majority of cases they ignore it entirely. The real situation was eloquently summed up at the recent New York life insurance investigation. It then appeared that at least one-third of the insured abandoned their policies, at great loss to themselves, after they have been in force for one or two years. Of those that are left two-thirds, at particular periods, surrender them, taking in exchange certain so-called "cash profits" and thus leaving their families unprovided for. In other words, out of every hundred only about twenty have entered the company for the insurance protection; or, if they have, have not yielded to the temptation of a cash reward and abandoned it.

If we wish mere life insurance unencumbered with modern improvements we must go to Connecticut, Massachusetts, New Jersey, and one or two other states. There we shall find great companies limiting their activities to one single end—the insuring of lives. They do not deal in investments, do not act as savings banks or lotteries. They collect from the insured during life certain stipulated sums, and, in the event of death, pay over to the widows certain equivalent indemnities. They collect from each member precisely the same pro rata price for the particular service rendered; and base this price upon certain well known mathematical laws which closely determine the exact cost. They treat all the insured upon a strictly "mutual basis," which, in the last analysis, means insurance at its actual cost and that actual cost to all. They furnish this article at a lower price than present quotations for the New York variety. They do it, too, without the elaborate machinery found so indispensable upon Manhattan Island. They have no subsidiary banks or trust companies; no string of office buildings stretched all over the civilized world; no alliance with captains of industry in Wall Street; no array of extravagantly salaried officers; no corruptionists in every important state capitol. They do not have enormous surpluses unjustly withheld from the policy-holders to whom they belong; do not pay in commissions for new business larger sums than that business is worth; do not write insurance in forty-five states and all foreign countries, including China, Japan, Borneo, and Malaysia; they remain quietly at home insuring only respectable heads of American families in good physical condition.

II
The Race for Bigness

The policy-holders have suffered most, not from the dishonesty of their trustees, but from their recklessness and extravagance. The amounts abstracted by underwriting syndicates and high salaries are insignificant compared with the millions wasted upon the agents. The overshadowing evil has been the craze for size. In the last thirty years the Mutual, the Equitable, and the New York Life have concentrated their energies upon a single end. They have aimed at leadership, not in providing the safest and fairest and lowest-cost life-insurance, but in writing the largest annual new business. They have aimed at quantity, not quality. They have become the most conspicuous illustration of the American passion for bigness. They have thus Barnumized the business. To this one fact the larger evils are directly traced.

These evils, outside of the actual dishonesty of the trustees, are the high cost of life-insurance and its frequently deceptive and fraudulent character. The high cost is explained by outrageous payments to agents, in the shape of commissions, prizes, bonuses, and miscellaneous forms of entertainment; by reckless advertising, rebates, and advances; and by the solicitation of business in foreign countries at the expense of the American members. Such expenditures, like most other details, are theoretically graded on a mathematical basis. Every policy-holder, as already explained, pays a certain "loading" on his premium each year as his contribution to management expenses. At age forty, for example, a $10,000 policy in the Equitable costs $330 a year. Of that, about $247 represents the actual cost of the insurance; and $82 the policy-holder's assessment for management expenses. Theoretically, the company expends as little of this loading as possible, and returns its savings in the shape of dividends—in other words, reduces, by that much, the cost of insurance. The connection between expenditures and the cost of life-insurance thus clearly appears. The company which manages its agency system with the greatest economy and thus makes the largest savings from "loadings" will return the largest dividends, or furnish insurance at the lowest cost. How grievously the New York companies have sinned, a few statistics will show. The New York Life, in 1903, spent $11,406,482 on the new business obtained that year. It collected in new premiums $13,784,000. In 1904 it spent $12,005,090 on new business; it collected in new premiums $13,988,186. The Equitable and the Mutual make a showing equally bad or worse. These three companies, that is, have much exceeded their entire loadings in management expenses,—notwithstanding the fact that their loadings are outrageously large. In other words, these companies have annually paid to agents, on new business, nearly ninety cents out of every dollar taken in. In many instances they have greatly overstepped this record. The Equitable, for example, has obtained its large English business by paying $1.25 for every dollar received in new premiums. In Australia it has paid out $1.40 for every dollar taken in.

READING NO. **11**

Samuel Hopkins Adams and The Great American Fraud*

Among those who fought against the patent medicines, with their false claims and their poisonous ingredients, were The Ladies Home Journal

* Samuel Hopkins Adams, "The Great American Fraud," *Collier's*, XXXVI (October 7, 1905), pp. 14–15, 29.

editor Edward Bok, lawyer-journalist Mark Sullivan, and government chemist Harvey Wiley. However, it was Samuel Hopkins Adams' Collier's Weekly *series in 1905–1906 that rallied public and legislative opinion for the battle to regulate food and drugs. The public and the politicians read Adams' articles on the patent medicines; the other journalists praised them; and the American Medical Association reprinted them and distributed them widely.*

Gullible America will spend this year some seventy-five millions of dollars in the purchase of patent medicines. In consideration of this sum it will swallow huge quantities of alcohol, an appalling amount of opiates and narcotics, a wide assortment of varied drugs ranging from powerful and dangerous heart depressants to insidious liver stimulants; and, far in excess of all other ingredients, undiluted fraud. For fraud exploited by the skillfulest of advertising bunco men, is the basis of the trade. Should the newspapers, the magazines and the medical journal refuse their pages to this class of advertisements, the patent medicine business in five years would be as scandalously historic as the South Sea Bubble, and the nation would be richer not only in lives and money, but in drunkards and drugfiends saved.

"Don't make the mistake of lumping all proprietary medicines in one indiscriminate denunciation," came warning from all sides when this series was announced. But the honest attempt to separate the sheep from the goats develops a lamentable lack of qualified candidates for the sheepfold. External remedies there may be which are at once honest in their claims and effective for their purposes; they are not to be found among the much-advertised ointments or applications which fill the public prints. Cuticura may be a useful preparation, but in extravagance of advertising it rivals the most clamorous cure-all. Pond's Extract, one would naturally suppose, could afford to restrict itself to decent methods, but in the recent epidemic scare in New York it traded on the public alarm by putting forth "display" advertisements headed, in heavy black type, "Meningitis," a disease in which witch-hazel is about as effective as molasses. This is fairly comparable to Peruna's ghoulish exploitation, for profit, of the yellow-fever scourge in New Orleans, aided by various southern newspapers of standing, which published as *news* an "interview" with Dr. Hartman, president of the Peruna Company.

Drugs That Make Victims

When one comes to the internal remedies, the proprietary medicines proper, they all belong to the tribe of Capricorn, under one of two heads, harmless frauds or deleterious drugs. For instance, the laxatives perform what they promise; but taken regularly, as thousands of people take them (and, indeed, as the advertisements urge), they become an increasingly baneful necessity. Acetanilid will undoubtedly relieve headache of certain kinds; but acetanilid, as the basis of headache powders, is prone to remove the cause of the symptoms permanently by putting a complete stop to the heart action. Invariably, when taken steadily, it produces constitutional disturbances of insidious develop- ment which result fatally if the drug be not discontinued, and often it enslaves the devotee to its use. Cocain and opium stop pain; but the narcotics are not the safest drugs to put into the hands of the ignorant, particularly when their presence is concealed in the "cough remedies," "soothing syrups," and "catarrh powders" of which they are the basis. Few outside of the rabid temperance advocates will deny a place in medical practice to alcohol. But alcohol, fed daily and in increasing doses to women and children, makes not for health, but for drunkenness. Far better whiskey or gin unequivocally labeled than the alcohol-laden "bitters," "sarsaparillas" and "tonics" which exhilarate fatuous temperance advocates to the point of enthusiastic testimo- nials.

None of these "cures" really does cure any serious affection, although a majority of their users recover. But a majority, and a very large majority, of the sick recover, anyway. Were it not so—were one illness out of fifty fatal—this earth would soon be depopulated. . . .

The Magic "Red Clause"

With a few honorable exceptions the press of the United States is at the beck and call of the patent medicines. Not only do the newspapers modify news possibly affecting these interests, but they sometimes become their active agents. F. J. Cheney, proprietor of Hall's Catarrh Cure, devised some years ago a method of making the press do his fighting against legislation compelling makers of remedies to publish their formulae, or to print on the labels the dangerous drugs contained in the medicine—a constantly recurring bugaboo of the nostrum-dealer. This scheme he unfolded at a meeting of the Proprietary Association of America, of which he is now president. He explained that he printed in red letters on every advertising contract a clause providing that the contract should become void in the event of hostile legislation, and he boasted how he had used this as a club in a case where an Illinois legislator had, as he put it, attempted to hold him for three hundred dollars on a strike bill.

"I thought I had a better plan than this," said Mr. Cheney to his associates, "so I wrote to about forty papers and merely said: 'Please look at your contract with me and take note that if this law passes you and I must stop doing business.' The next week every one of them had an article and Mr. Man had to go."

So emphatically did this device recommend itself to the assemblage that many of the large firms took up the plan, and now the "red clause" is a familiar device in the trade. The reproduction printed on page 6 is a fac-simile of a contract between Mr. Cheney's firm and the Emporia *Gazette*, William Allen White's paper, which has since become one of the newspapers to abjure the patent-medicine man and all his ways. Emboldened by this easy coercion of the press, certain firms have since used the newspapers as a weapon against "price-cutting," by forcing them to refuse advertising of the stores which reduce rates on patent medicines. Tyrannical masters, these heavy purchasers of advertising space. . . .

One might expect from the medical press freedom from such influences. The control is as complete, though exercised by a class of nostrums somewhat differently exploited, but essentially the same. Only "ethical" preparations are permitted in the representative medical press, that is, articles not advertised in the lay press. Yet this distinction is not strictly adhered to. "Syrup of Figs," for instance, which makes widespread pretense in the dailies to be an extract of the fig, advertises in the medical journals for what it is, a preparation of senna. Antikamnia, an "ethical" proprietary compound, for a long time exploited itself to the profession by a campaign of ridiculous extravagance, and is to-day by the extent of its reckless use on the part of ignorant laymen a public menace. Recently an article announcing a startling new drug discovery and signed by a physician was offered to a standard medical journal, which declined it on learning that the drug was a proprietary preparation. The contribution was returned to the editor with an offer of payment at advertising rates if it were printed as editorial reading matter, only to be rejected on the new basis. Subsequently it appeared simultaneously in more than twenty medical publications as reading matter. There are to-day very few medical publications which do not carry advertisements conceived in the same spirit and making much the same exhaustive claims as the ordinary quack "ads" of the daily press, and still fewer that are free from promises to "cure" diseases which are incurable by any medicine. Thus the medical press is as strongly enmeshed by the "ethical" druggers as the lay press is by Paine, "Dr." Kilmer, Lydia Pinkham, Dr. Hartman, "Hall" of the "red clause," and the rest of the edifying band of life-savers, leaving no agency to refute the megaphone exploitation of the fraud. What opposition there is would naturally arise in the medical profession, but this is discounted by the proprietary interests. . . .

The physicians seem to have awakened, somewhat tardily, indeed, to counter-attack. The American Medical Association has organized a Council on Pharmacy and Chemistry to investigate and pass on the "ethical" preparations advertised to physicians, with a view to listing those which are found to be reputable and useful. That this is regarded as a direct assault on the proprietary interests is suggested by the protests, eloquent to the verge of frenzy in some cases, emanating from those organs which the manufacturers control. Already the council has issued some painfully frank reports on products of imposingly scientific nomenclature; and more are to follow. . . .

Legislation is the most obvious remedy, pending the enlightenment of the general public or the awakening of the journalistic conscience. But legislation proceeds slowly and always against opposition, which may be measured in practical terms as $250,000,000 at stake on the other side. I note in the last report of the Proprietary Association's annual meeting the significant statement that "the heaviest expenses were incurred in legislative work." Most of the legislation must be done by states, and we have seen in the case of the Hall Catarrh cure contract how readily this may be controlled.

Two government agencies, at least, lend themselves to the purposes of the patent-medicine makers. The Patent Office issues to them trade-mark registration (generally speaking, the convenient term "patent medicine" is a misnomer, as very few are patented) without inquiry into the nature of the article thus safeguarded against imitation. The Post-Office Department permits them the use of the mails. Except one particular line, the disgraceful "Weak Manhood" remedies, where excellent work has been done in throwing them out of the mails for fraud, the department has done nothing in the matter of patent remedies, and has no present intention of doing anything. . . .

Some states have made a good start in the matter of legislation, among them Michigan, which does not, however, enforce its recent strong law. Massachusetts, which has done more, through the admirable work of its State Board of Health, than any other agency to educate the public on the patent-medicine question, is unable to get a law restricting this trade. In New Hampshire, too, the proprietary interests have proven too strong, and the Mallonee bill was destroyed by the almost united opposition of a "red-clause" press. North Dakota proved more independent. After Jan. 1, 1906, all medicines sold in that state, except on physician's prescriptions, which contain chloral, ergot, morphin, opium, cocain, bromin, iodin or any of their compounds or derivatives, or more than 5 per cent. of alcohol, must so state on the label. When this bill became a law, the Proprietary Association of America proceeded to blight the state by resolving that its members should offer no goods for sale there.

Boards of health in various parts of the country are doing valuable educational work, the North Dakota board having led in the legislation. The Massachusetts, Connecticut and North Carolina boards have been active. The New York State board has kept its hands off patent medicines, but the Board of Pharmacy has made a cautious but promising beginning by compelling all makers of powders containing cocain to put a poison label on their goods; and it proposes to extend this ruling gradually to other dangerous compositions. . . .

It is impossible, even in a series of articles, to attempt more than an exemplary treatment of the patent-medicine frauds. The most degraded and degrading, the "lost vitality" and "blood disease" cures, reeking of terrorization and blackmail, cannot from their very nature be treated of in a lay journal. Many dangerous and health-destroying compounds will escape through sheer inconspicuousness. I can touch on only a few of those which may be regarded as typical: the alcohol stimulators, as represented by Peruna, Paine's Celery Compound and Duffy's Pure Malt Whiskey (advertised as an exclusively medical preparation); the catarrh powders, which breed cocain slaves, and the opium-containing soothing syrups which stunt or kill helpless infants; the consumption cures, perhaps the most devilish of all, in that they destroy hope where hope is struggling against bitter odds for existence; the headache powders, which enslave so insidiously that the victim is ignorant of his own fate; the comparatively harmless fake as typified by that marvelous product of advertising effrontery, Liquozone; and, finally, the system of exploitation and testimonials on which the whole vast system of bunco rests, as on a flimsy but cunningly constructed foundation.

READING NO. 12

The Jungle*

Upton Sinclair's socialist novel about the immigrant workers in the Chicago packing houses first appeared serially in the radical Appeal to

* Upton Sinclair, *The Jungle* (New York, 1906), pp. 160–162.

Reason. *When Sinclair was finally able to get Doubleday, Page and Company to publish it as a book, it was an explosive sensation. It helped push meat inspection and drug and railroad legislation through Congress, but fell far short of producing Sinclair's hoped for social revolution.*

With one member trimming beef in a cannery, and another working in a sausage factory, the family had a first-hand knowledge of the great majority of Packingtown swindles. For it was the custom, as they found, whenever meat was so spoiled that it could not be used for anything else, either to can it or else to chop it up into sausage. With what had been told them by Jonas, who had worked in the pickle-rooms, they could now study the whole of the spoiled-meat industry on the inside, and read a new and grim meaning into that old Packingtown jest,—that they use everything of the pig except the squeal.

Jonas had told them how the meat that was taken out of pickle would often be found sour, and how they would rub it up with soda to take away the smell, and sell it to be eaten on free-lunch counters; also of all the miracles of chemistry which they performed, giving to any sort of meat, fresh or salted, whole or chopped, any color and any flavor and any odor they chose. In the pickling of hams they had an ingenious apparatus, by which they saved time and increased the capacity of the plant—a machine consisting of a hollow needle attached to a pump; by plunging this needle into the meat and working with his foot, a man could fill a ham with pickle in a few seconds. And yet, in spite of this, there would be hams found spoiled, some of them with an odor so bad that a man could hardly bear to be in the room with them. To pump into these the packers had a second and much stronger pickle which destroyed the odor—a process known to the workers as "giving them thirty per cent." Also, after the hams had been smoked, there would be found some that had gone to the bad. Formerly these had been sold as "Number Three Grade," but later on some ingenious person had hit upon a new device, and now they would extract the bone, about which the bad part generally lay, and insert in the hole a white-hot iron. After this invention there was no longer Number One, Two, and Three Grade—there was only Number One Grade. The packers were always originating such schemes—they had what they called "boneless hams," which were all the odds and ends of pork stuffed into casings; and "California hams," which were the shoulders with big knuckle-joints, and nearly all the meat cut out; and fancy "skinned hams," which were made of the oldest hogs, whose skins were so heavy and coarse that no one would buy them—that is, until they had been cooked and chopped fine and labelled "head cheese"!

It was only when the whole ham was spoiled that it came into the department of Elzbieta. Cut up by the two-thousand-revolutions-a-minute flyers, and mixed with half a ton of other meat, no odor that ever was in a ham could make any difference. There was never the least attention paid to what was cut up for sausage; there would come all the way back from Europe old sausage that had been rejected, and that was mouldy and white—it would be dosed with borax and glycerine, and dumped into the hoppers, and made over again for home consumption. There would be meat that had tumbled out on the floor, in the dirt and sawdust, where the workers had tramped and spit uncounted billions of consumption germs. There would be meat stored in great piles in rooms; and the water from leaky roofs would drip over it, and thousands of rats would race about on it. It was too dark in these storage places to see well, but a man could run his hand over these piles of meat and sweep off handfuls of the dried dung of rats. These rats were nuisances, and the packers would put poisoned bread out for them; they would die, and then rats, bread, and meat would go into the hoppers together. This is no fairy story and no joke; the meat would be shovelled into carts, and the man who did the shovelling would not trouble to lift out a rat even when he saw one—there were things that went into the sausage in comparison with which a poisoned rat was a tidbit. There was no place for the men to wash their hands before they ate their dinner, and so they made a practice of washing them in the water that was to be ladled into the sausage. There were the butt-ends of smoked meat, and the scraps of corned beef, and all the odds and ends of the waste of the plants, that would be dumped into old barrels in the cellar and left there. Under the system of rigid economy which the packers enforced, there were some jobs that it only paid to do once in a long time, and among these was the cleaning out of the waste-barrels. Every spring they did it; and in the barrels would be dirt and rust and old nails and stale water—and cart load after cart load of it would be taken up and dumped into the hoppers with fresh meat, and sent out to the public's breakfast. Some of it they would make into "smoked" sausage—but as the smoking took time, and was therefore expensive, they would call upon their chemistry department, and preserve it with borax and color it with gelatine to make it brown. All of their sausage came out of the same bowl, but when they came to wrap it they would stamp some of it "special," and for this they would charge two cents more a pound.

READING NO. **13**

The Demand for Clean Meat*

Upton Sinclair's packingtown novel, The Jungle, *was a sensation. It led to denials, cover-ups, controversy, and a popular demand for action to supervise and regulate the meat industry. The unsanitary handling of meat in the packing houses stayed in the headlines and on the editorial pages. The* Literary Digest *offered a running summary of the arguments, listed in each issue under the heading "Topics of the Day."* Collier's Weekly *published a satire on the meat industry by Finley Peter Dunne in which he described an Irish saloon-keeper, Mr. Dooley, explaining to his friend Mr. Hennessy the dangers of eating meat.*

I

DEMAND FOR CLEAN MEAT.

The substantiation, in the main, of Upton Sinclair's terrible allegations in "The Jungle" by the Neill-Reynolds report on the Chicago packing-house evils has roused an imperative demand by the press for instant and thoroughgoing reformation. Messrs. Neill and Reynolds could not confirm some of the more revolting details of the loss of human life, but the descriptions of uncleanliness, unsanitary features, and the evil of conditions generally are pretty well established. With typical American impetuosity the newspapers demand immediate action on the part of Congress and the President. Chicago, the heart and center of the packing industry and home of the Union Stockyards, feels, in the words of the Chicago *Record-Herald*, "the need of a full exposition of the conditions there, and would welcome such regulations as would be a guaranty against abuses." To quote further:

"It can emphatically indorse a provision of the Beveridge bill that all establishments in which cattle, sheep, or swine are slaughtered and the

---

* I. "Demand for Clean Meat," *The Literary Digest*, XXXII (June 9, 1906), pp. 859—860. II. Finley Peter Dunne, "The Food We Eat," *Collier's Weekly*, XXXVII (June 23, 1906), p. 15.

meat and food products are prepared for interstate and foreign commerce shall be maintained in a sanitary manner, according to rules to be prescribed by the Secretary of Agriculture. Not only has it much to gain and nothing to lose by thoroughly adequate inspection, but it is keenly alive to the rights of meat consumers in the matter of sanitation. For the subject is one that concerns both its own people and its own fame.

"And what is to the interest of the city is to the interest of the packers also. Their best defense lies not in fighting regulation, but in inviting it. The great packers, in particular, could pursue no more disastrous policy than one of resistance and defiance. While it is a fact that conditions may be better in their establishments than in the smaller ones, they must bear the brunt of the charges, and their sole aim should be to make good for themselves regardless of others. They must realize that it is on them that the interest of the whole American public is centered, and that Chicago is in no mood to share the odium that may attach to them from stock-yards scandals."

It is, thinks the Chicago *News*, "a sign of progress that the outcry against Socialistic tendencies has ceased to influence the public when a measure of necessary regulation is brought forward." The country, under the President's leadership, in the belief of *The News*, "is striving, by means of government supervision, to establish a proper balance between individual activities on a large scale and the public's interest. This is not a drift into Socialism, but such progress in government as the evolution of modern business methods has rendered necessary and desirable." The Chicago *Inter Ocean*, however, feels that the entire business has been greatly exaggerated. It asks what the present United States inspectors in the packing-houses are for, "and why have we inspection laws?" It continues:

"The remedy is as plain as are the only possible explanations. It is for executive authority, if possible, and, if not, for legislative authority, to change either the system or the men, or both.

"To insist merely that more men shall be hired, more money spent out of hand, and the whole cattle industry be burdened, without first making sure that the system is right and the men now working it are doing their duty, is but to repeat the folly recently perpetrated here in enlarging our inefficient police force.

"This whole question is one merely of the present government inspectors doing their duty intelligently. It is no question of fireworks.

"Do they do it or don't they? And, if not, how can they be made to do it? That's all.

"It is of evident advantage to settle these plain business questions plainly and without hysterics. Melodrama has nothing to do with meat inspection. Neither has novel-writing."

But the majority of the press in beef-packing centers are otherwise minded. The Kansas City *Times*, for instance, is of the opinion that in his present movement the President will have "the sympathy and cooperation of the people as he has had these helps in his other reforms," and it makes this suggestion:

"Every city, at least, should have a system that would enable the authorities to inspect all markets and restaurants thoroughly, condemn spoiled or unclean foods and, in cases of culpable negligence or adulteration, enforce heavy penalties. It would not take a large army of inspectors to regulate a city, if those employed were vigilant and had a good law back of them. So long as a dealer is liable any day to a visit from an inspector with authority to go through his establishment, he will come pretty near keeping himself in readiness for such visits."

The curious negligence of the existing law which compels inspection only of export beef and leaves the product for home consumption unprovided for has called forth the indignation of most of the large cities. Indeed, the cities are crying out upon each other. In the opinion of the New York *World*, "whatever crimes the packers have committed against the public health, Chicago and Illinois are accessaries both before and after the fact." With regard to New York *The World* says:

"Not more inspectors, but the enforcement of the existing law, is the remedy for any evils in local packing-houses. There are six inspectors now. Dr. Darlington asks for fifty more. What have the six done? Has any one of them in the past year secured a conviction of a packer for the violation of section 408 of the Penal Code, which says:

"A person who with intent that the same may be used as food, drink, or medicine, sells or offers or exposes for sale any article whatever which to his knowledge is tainted or spoiled or for any cause unfit to be used as such food, drink, or medicine, is guilty of a misdemeanor.

"There are only a few abattoirs and packing-houses in Greater New York. One conviction even would be an example to all the rest. There should be no substitution of municipal responsibility for the individual liability now existing under the present comprehensive law."

We are all, in the words of the New York *Evening Post*, "easily excited about what we eat," and that is why the press urge full publication of all the facts. In the interval of waiting for these facts, *The Post* thinks, "millions of people must already have vowed that never again will they touch canned meats or by-products of the slaughter-house in any form."

II
THE FOOD WE EAT

"What have ye undher ye'er arm there?" demanded Mr. Dooley.

"I was takin' home a ham," said Mr. Hennessy.

"Clear out iv here with it," cried Mr. Dooley. "Take that thing outside—an' don't lave it where th' dog might get hold iv it. Th' idee iv ye'er bringin' it in here! Glory be, it makes me faint to think iv it. I'm afraid I'll have to go an' lay down."

"What ails ye?" asked Mr. Hennessy.

"What ails me?" said Mr. Dooley. "Haven't ye r-read about th' invistygation iv th' Stock Yards? It's a good thing f'r ye ye haven't. If ye knew what that ham—oh, th' horrid wurrud—was made iv ye'd go down to Rabbi Hirsch an' be baptized f'r a Jew.

"Ye may think 'tis th' innocint little last left leg iv a porker ye're inthrajoocin' into ye'er innocint fam'ly, but I tell ye, me boy, th' pig that that ham was cut fr'm has as manny legs to-day as iver he had. Why did ye waste ye'er good money on it? Why didn't ye get th' fam'ly into th' dining-room, shut th' windows, an' turn on th' gas? I'll be readin' in th' pa-aper to-morrah that wan Hinnissy took an overdose iv Unblemished Ham with suicidal intint an' died in gr-reat agony. Take it away! It's lible to blow up at anny minyit, scattherin' death an' desthruction in its train.

"Dear, oh dear, I haven't been able to ate annything more nourishin' thin a cucumber in a week. I'm grajally fadin' fr'm life. A little while ago no wan cud square away at a beefsteak with betther grace thin mesilf. To-day th' wurrud resthrant makes me green in th' face. How did it all come about? A young fellow wrote a book. Th' divvle take him f'r writin' it. Hogan says it's a grand book. It's wan iv th' gr-reatest books he iver r-read. It almost made him commit suicide. Th' hero is a Lithuanian, or as ye might say, Pollacky, who left th' barb'rous land iv his birth an' come to this home iv opporchunity were ivry man is th' equal iv ivry other man befure th' law if he isn't careful. Our hero got a fancy job poling food products out iv a catch-basin, an' was promoted to scrapin' pure leaflard off th' flure iv th' glue facthry. But th' binifits iv our gloryous civilyzation were wasted on this poor peasant. Instead iv bein' thankful f'r what he got, an' lookin' forward to a day whin his opporchunity wud arrive an', be merely stubbin' his toe, he might become rich an' famous as a pop'lar soup, he grew cross an' unruly, bit his boss, an' was sint to jail. But it all tur-rned out well in th' end. Th' villain fell into a lard-tank an' was not seen again ontil he tur-rned up at a fash'nable resthrant in New York. Our hero got out iv jail an' was rewarded with a pleasant position as a porter iv an arnychist hotel, an' all ended merry as a fun'ral bell.

"Ye'll see be this that 'tis a sweetly sintimintal little volume to be r-read durin' Lent. It's had a grand success, an' I'm glad iv it. I see be th' publishers' announcemints that 'tis th' gr-reatest lithry hog-killin' in a peryod iv gin'ral lithry culture. If ye want to rayjooce ye'er butcher's bills buy *Th' Jungle*. . . .

"Well, sir, it put th' Prisidint in a tur-rble stew. Oh, Lawd, why did I say that? Think iv—but I mustn't go on. Annyhow, Tiddy was toying with a light breakfast an' idly turnin' over th' pages iv th' new book with both hands. Suddenly he rose fr'm th' table, an' cryin': 'I'm pizened,' begun throwin' sausages out iv th' window. Th' ninth wan sthruck Sinitor Biv'ridge on th' head an' made him a blond. It bounced off, exploded, an' blew a leg off a secret-service agent, an' th' scatthred fragmints desthroyed a handsome row iv ol' oak-trees. Sinitor Biv'ridge rushed in, thinkin' that th' Prisidint was bein' assassynated be his devoted followers in th' Sinit, an' discovered Tiddy engaged in a hand-to-hand conflict with a potted ham. Th' Sinitor fr'm Injyanny, with a few well-directed wurruds, put out th' fuse an' rendered th' missile harmless. Since thin th' Prisidint, like th' rest iv us, has become a viggytaryan. . . .

"They ought to make thim ate their own meat," said Mr. Hennessy, warmly.

"I suggested that," said Mr. Dooley, "but Hogan says they'd fall back on th' Constitution. He says th' Constitution f'rbids crool an' unusual punishmints."

READING NO. **14**

Charles Edward Russell's Soldiers of the Common Good*

Charles Edward Russell came into the business of exposure with a well-established reputation as a newspaperman and editor. After Every-body's *persuaded him to write on the beef trust, the magazine sent him on a round-the-world trip to study social conditions and remedies in other countries. From his articles it is obvious that Russell was well along the way to socialism, and in 1908 he formally joined the party.*

* Charles Edward Russell, "Soldiers of the Common Good," *Every-body's*, XIV (February, 1906), pp. 180–181, 184–185; (April, 1906), pp. 477–479; XV (October, 1906), p. 499; (December, 1906), pp. 791–792.

We have in America a pleasing way of assuming that the Government of Germany operates the German railroads because the spirit of enterprise and achievement is lacking among the German people; the Government, we Americans think, must needs do these things because private individuals don't know how; and this in spite of the fact that German enterprise has conceived and carried on commercial undertakings as great and daring as anything we ever dreamed of. The truth is that in the beginning all the German railroads were privately owned, and until thirty-five years ago nobody in Germany supposed there would ever be any other kind of ownership. *The Government woke up in 1871 to recognize two facts—first, that whoever owns a country's transportation service owns the country; and second, that it needed the national highways for national use.* The war with France first jolted the private ownership idea, for the Government had found the railroad companies exorbitant, unreasonable, and given to grafting when it came to transporting troops and supplies, but we also had our share in effecting the transformation. It was the time of Tom Scott, the Pennsylvania monopoly, Jay Gould, the wrecking of Erie, the beginning of legislative bribery as a fine art. No important development or manifestation around the world escapes the hawk-like watching of the German Government. Tom Scott's performances were known and understood in Berlin as thoroughly as ever they were known in New York. The appearance of a new factor in Government able to control legislatures, nullify laws, and operate illimitable schemes of public plunder made a strong impression on the German mind. Moreover, much German capital had gone into American railroads about that time and very little had come out, and following its dizzy revolutions through debenture bonds, consolidated mortgages, equipment bonds, common, preferred and hocus-pocus issues, and the vast and sailless ocean of watered stock, showed the Germans some highly disagreeable possibilities of the private system. So the Government determined as a matter of safety to run the railroads on its own account. . . .

The annual passenger traffic on the German railroad is about 900,000,000 persons. More than half of these travel third class and thirty-three per cent. travel fourth class; eighty-eight per cent. of the passenger traffic is represented in these two classes and less than one per cent. in the first class, so essentially is the railroad a thing for poor people. The average distance traveled is twenty miles for each person. The annual freight tonnage of the German railroads is about 400,000,000 tons. The railroads employ 550,000 persons, pay $187,500,000 a year in wages, $700,000 a year in pensions to old employees, $350,000 a year to the widows of employees, and $15,000 a year for the burial of employees. *So far as any outsider can discover there is no grafting—and assuredly there is no stock juggling, bond juggling, rate juggling, rebates, discriminations, thefts, underbilling, wrong classifications, skin games, and frauds on shippers. Every shipper knows exactly what he pays and what his competitors pay, and the chief plaint of the American shipper is absolutely unknown in Germany.*

On the whole, though comparisons are difficult, freight rates seem somewhat higher in Germany than in America, varying from one cent a mile for a ton to two and one-half cents, whereas the bulk of American freight traffic goes at from .61 cents to 2.08 cents a mile for a ton. But the differences in classification tend to equalize all this. The German tariff is very much simpler than ours. There are not one thousand items in the German classification list, and with us the Western classification alone has 8,044 items, the Southern 3,664, and the American Official 9,370.

Moreover, the German shipper has three great advantages over the American. In the first place, the German rates never change; the American rates go up and down with the exigencies of the only American rule for rate-making, which in railroad parlance is "the last cent the people will stand without rioting." In the next place the rates are absolutely the same to everybody, rich and poor, trust or no trust, campaign subscriber or peasant, Ogden Armour or Hans Schmidt—the rates are the same. In the next place there is nobody in Germany sneaking about at night with money under his hat lining, dealing out rebates—as there is in every American shipping center. . . .

The German railroad system is not complicated by any rebate issues, nor by lobbies, pools, combinations, dark-lantern deals, secret compacts, crooked Congressmen, purchased Senators, bribed District Attorneys. No part of the railroad earnings in Germany need be set apart for the expenses of gentlemen engaged in manipulating political conventions, or in electing certain candidates and defeating certain others. That makes a wonderful difference in the practical operations of the system and a wonderful advantage to the public pocketbook. In Germany railroad rates are based on the cost of transportation, the interest on the outstanding bonds, and a fair profit on the service performed. In America they are based on the traffic manager's nerve. That makes some difference. . . .

I have spoken of the admirable traction system of Zurich. The lines comprise in all twenty-five and one-half miles of trackage. The receipts in 1904 were $343,850 on which the city profits were $138,095. Of these profits $19,000 went to a surplus fund for renewals, $10,000 to the sinking-fund to meet the purchase bonds, $63,258 to pay the interest on these obligations, and $45,837 was turned into the general funds of the city—"for the Common Good," as the Zurich people express it. The lines carried in 1904 14,297,000 persons, an increase of one million over

1903. The total sum paid for damages resulting from accidents to others than employees was $237. To injured workmen on its lines the city paid $2,000. No suits were necessary to enforce these claims; they were paid because they were just. No politics entered into the conduct of the road. All the details of its operations, the receipts and expenditures to the last centime were published in pamphlets. Every citizen of Zurich could know as much as the manager about the finances of the lines.

This brings me naturally to the next reason why the Swiss do so well. Everything done by their Government is done out in the daylight; they can know all about it if they wish. And the Government makes sure that if it practises no hugger-mugger itself it allows no one else to practise hugger-mugger either. Its hand is upon every corporation, big or little, public or private, that transacts a dollar's worth of business in Switzerland. Every Swiss corporation must publish at regular intervals in each year a detailed and exact statement of its condition, the amount of business it has transacted, its profits and the disposition thereof—all in plain black and white. The penalties for juggling with the figures are such that corporations do not dare to lie; for in Switzerland no distinctions are drawn between corporation rascality and individual rascality, and the officers are held personally responsible for the corporation's acts. The Government provides an official periodical for these reports; no stock company can escape its columns. *Moreover, a corporation in Switzerland has no chance to play tricks on its stockholders. Any two stockholders can at any time demand to see the books or know anything they wish to know about the concern. If a corporation should refuse the information, the stockholders would go into court and the court would in an hour have the whole thing into the sunlight and some of its officers on the road to jail.* In Switzerland they know what corporations are and take no chances. They say they have no intention of being throttled by that particular constrictor, anyway. . . .

Insurance scandals and swindles such as we have recently been regaled with could never occur in Switzerland. This Government looks upon insurance as a thing vitally concerning most of its citizens and to be watched lest the public interests suffer. Therefore, it keeps the insurance companies under incessant supervision and inspection. They must show what they do with their money, and if they fall to fooling with their reserves and surpluses, out they go from Switzerland. There are no profitable "side syndicates" for insurance directors here, no stock pools, no checks for Mr. Depew, no dinners for actresses, no campaign subscriptions. The Government would instantly detect the missing money and demand to know about it. Foreign insurance companies doing business in Switzerland must make regular returns of all the policies they issue and invest a certain proportion of the total in Swiss property, and this property the Government is prepared to confiscate at any time for the benefit of the policy-holders.

Again, this Government does not allow gentlemen to make great fortunes by selling things unfit for food—poisoned meat, for instance. No Beef Trust could ever exist in Switzerland, nor any private interference with the food-supply, for the simple reason that the Government does all the slaughtering in its own slaughter-houses under its own sanitary supervision. No private person is allowed to slaughter animals for food. Those interested in the subject may care to know that no "lumpy jaw" cattle are eaten in Switzerland, and few Swiss have cancer. On the whole, the Swiss seem to have rather the best of us in this regard. I recall the grisly secrets of Chicago Packingtown, the doors behind which no one is allowed to go, the horrible filth, the "lumpy jaw" cattle, and the swine with tuberculosis that go somewhere and do not return—the hideous revelations of the London *Lancet*. Are we quite sure we can teach everything to the Swiss? At least they know, when they sit down to dinner, that they are not to eat cancer germs, nor infected pork, nor the flesh of animals that have died natural deaths. They also know that they are not paying artificial tribute to private fortunes. Suppose the State of Illinois owned and operated all the slaughter-houses within its borders. How long would the American Beef Trust last? Five minutes? . . .

President Roosevelt could never persuade the people of Western Australia that the government ownership of railroads is "the greatest misfortune that can befall a nation," because they have had practical experience with a misfortune much greater. Once all their railroads were owned by private companies. There is no consideration that could induce them to return to that kind of ownership. A chapter from the history of their experiences will show why no consideration could induce the people of Western Australia to return to private ownership.

Before 1899 the Great Southern Railroad from Beverly to Albany, 243 miles, was private property, and even for a railroad operated solely for dividends the service it furnished seems to have been bad. Settlers complained incessantly of extortionate charges and arbitrary treatment. They used to exhibit tariff sheets showing that when the season had been good and the crops abundant, the company advanced the rates so that good harvests really meant nothing except to the railroad. I suppose that I need hardly say that the rates thus advanced were never afterward reduced. To reduce them would not be in accordance with railroad companies' practise all over the world. In Australia as easily as in America the companies worked the old humbug game about the vast mystery and difficulty of making railroad rates, and while they juggled like prestidigitators the rates always went up. Substantial demonstration of the justice of the settlers' complaints was found in the fact that in ten years the region showed practically no gains in population. There is nothing to tempt newcomers in a region where all the profits of the undertaking are skimmed off by the railroads. Tradesmen as well as farmers complained; they had to submit to extortion on their freight shipped in as much as the farmer was robbed on his freight shipped out. Of course the railroad was owned in England, and its resident managers, like the managers of the Irish railroads similarly owned, had no business and no responsibility except to gouge profits and to show dividends. So in 1899 the exasperated government determined to end a situation it had tried in vain to control, and bought outright the whole enterprise. Since then the railroad has been operated for the Common Good. One of the results has been that the settlers have had lower rates for their produce and better service. Another has been that in the seven years since the purchase the population in that region has quadrupled. And another has been that with increased service and lower rates the government has still made a profit on the investment. . . .

There never can be in New Zealand any Coal Trust nor any manipulation of the coal market, nor any coal shortage to rig stocks, nor robber prices for coal, because the government owns and operates great coal-mines for the Common Good, and keeps up the public supply while it keeps down the price. Even at the moderate charge it makes, the government reaps an agreeable profit from its coal-mining operations. In its mines at Point Elizabeth and Seddonville its investment is $320,906, on which it made last year a profit of $55,212. After all deductions and charges this left a net profit of eight per cent. on the investment. Originally the intention was to use these mines as a check on the greed of private mining companies, but within the last three or four months the government has scattered its sale agents through the towns and villages, reduced the price of coal, enlarged its output, and seems now on the way to absorb the entire coal business of the country—just as the government of Japan absorbed the tobacco business, and other things, you may remember.

In New Zealand there can never be any railroad rebates, secret rate-making, cut-throat discriminations, terminal railroad frauds, thievish switching charges, nor swindling private-car graft; and in New Zealand the railroads can never be used to build up any "Systems" nor Standard Oil Companies nor Beef Trusts nor any other piracies, because the government owns or practically controls all the railroads, and operates them on one flat flint basis of equal, uniform, and invariable rates. . . .

We are accustomed to think that about railroad rate-making there is some strange and awful mystery, that to make railroad rates a man must go into a trance and commune with spirits or something like that, and that if the government should ever try to fix the rates, frightful convulsions of nature would follow. They do not seem to have such fears in New Zealand. There the government makes all the rates. In plain daylight Mr. Cassatt. On a mileage basis. All a shipper has to do is to calculate his mileage and he has his rate. If he can show that either of the private companies has charged him more than the rate on a government railroad for the same distance, he can go into court and collect the difference. In about ten minutes. . . .

READING NO. 15

Ray Stannard Baker and Railroads on Trial *

By the time he finished writing his series on the railroads, Ray Stannard Baker was seriously considering the need for government ownership. However, in his articles on the consequences of railroad discrimination, Baker sought to make the case for national regulation. Theodore Roosevelt was one of his most careful readers.

Shrewd men in Danville, as everywhere else, recognized transportation facilities as the key of industry and the chief cause of city growth. In every part of the country during the 70's and 80's the people were mortgaging their cities and counties to help private railroad builders. When the Virginia Midland road was projected, to run from Washington City to Danville, the citizens, eager for this new outlet into Northern markets, contributed no less than $400,000. in cash ($100,000. by the city, $300,000. by Pittsylvania county), to the projectors of the enterprise. When the road was completed in 1874, Danville immediately felt its vivifying effects. The town grew rapidly both in population and in wealth.

If such was the effect of railroads, said Danville, why not have more of them? The reasoning seemed good, and when the Danville & Western was projected in the 80's to run to the coal-fields, (where it never arrived)

* Ray Stannard Baker, "The Way Of A Railroad With A Town," *McClure's*, XXVII (June, 1906), pp. 134, 145.

the city cheerfully presented the private builders with $110,000. in cash. In these years of free competition the town outstripped its rival to the north and became a thriving commercial center.

By this time the country was reaching the era of combinations, consolidations, and trusts. Short railroad lines were being connected under single ownerships. Great trunk lines took form. And one day in 1886, Danville awakened to the discovery that its two competing railroads—its only outlet to the markets of the world—had been swallowed up in the system afterwards known as the Southern Railway, which now spreads a network of lines from Washington to the Gulf of Mexico and the Mississippi River.

Danville thus found itself in 1887 at the mercy of a railroad monopoly; the competition which had been the life of its trade has wholly disappeared. . . .

I have thus endeavored to give a clear idea of what conditions are in Danville. A few points in conclusion should be emphasized.

Is it right that the Southern Railway, having a monopoly, should charge high rates at Danville to make up for the low competitive rates at Lynchburg? Should Danville help to pay Lynchburg's freight rates? The Southern Railway admits making a profit on its Lynchburg business, even at the low competitive rates: why, then, should Danville be required to pay from thirty to one hundred per cent more profit?

Is it right that the very life of a town in Virginia should be in the hands of private individuals in New York city or elsewhere, who have no sympathy with Danville, and are working, not for justice, but for private profit?

Railroads are public highways which all people have a right to use upon equal terms. Is it right for the Southern Railway, upon any excuse whatever, to deny the people of Danville this equality upon the public highway?

Is it right that the Southern Railway having deprived Danville of competition should now plead its own wrong in defense of high rates at Danville and low rates at Lynchburg? If the beggar on the streets has no right to steal money because he is a beggar, has the Southern Railway a right to do a wrong merely because it needs revenue?

Is it right that a railroad which objects so strongly to the confiscation of its property, should be allowed to depreciate the value of property in towns where it has a monopoly?

The railroad says that such adjustments as those between Lynchburg and Danville are fixed by competitory conditions beyond its control. If the railroad cannot itself cure such injustice, why should not the governmental commission be empowered to do it?

Is it right, finally, that there should be no power in this country strong enough to prevent railroad injustice and railroad discriminations like those existing in Danville?

READING NO. 16

David Graham Phillips and The Treason of the Senate*

The politically ambitious publisher-congressman William Randolph Hearst bought Cosmopolitan *and used it to print the most far reaching and sensationalistic of the era's exposures, "The Treason of the Senate." David Graham Phillips did the writing and argued that the Senate of the United States was betraying the people through subservience to the big business "interests." It was this series that prompted President Theodore Roosevelt to apply the label of "muck-rakers" to the journalists.*

When Aldrich entered the Senate, twenty-five years ago, at the splendid full age of forty, the world was just beginning to feel the effects of the principles of concentration and combination, which were inexorably and permanently established with the discoveries in steam and electricity that make the whole human race more and more like one community of interdependent neighbors. It was a moment of opportunity, an unprecedented chance for Congress, especially its deliberate and supposedly sagacious senators, to "promote the general welfare" by giving those principles free and just play in securing the benefits of expanding prosperity to all, by seeing that the profits from the cooperation of all the people went *to* the people. Aldrich and the traitor Senate saw the opportunity. But they saw in it only a chance to enable a class to despoil the masses. . . .

Various senators represent various divisions and subdivisions of this colossus. But Aldrich, rich through franchise grabbing, the intimate of Wall Street's great robber barons, the father-in-law of the only son of *the* Rockefeller—Aldrich represents the colossus. Your first impression of

* David Graham Phillips, "The Treason of the Senate," *Cosmopolitan*, XL (April, 1906), pp. 631–634, 636.

many and conflicting interests has disappeared. You now see a single interest, with a single agent-in-chief to execute its single purpose—getting rich at the expense of the labor and the independence of the American people. And the largest head among the many heads of this monster is that of Rockefeller, father of the only son-in-law of Aldrich and his intimate in all the relations of life!

There are many passages in the Constitution in which a Senate, true to its oath and mindful of the welfare of the people and of the nation, could find mandates to stop wholesale robbery, and similar practices.

And yet, what has the Senate done—the Senate, with its high-flown pretenses of reverence for the Constitution? It has so legislated and so refrained from legislating that more than half of all the wealth created by the American people belongs to less than one per cent of them; that the income of the average American family has sunk to less than six hundred dollars a year; that of our more than twenty-seven million children of school age, less than twelve millions go to school, and more than two millions work in mines, shops and factories.

And the leader, the boss of the Senate for the past twenty years has been—Aldrich!

In vain would "the interests" have stolen franchises, in vain would they have corrupted the public officials of states and cities, if they had not got absolute and unshakable control of the Senate. But, with the Senate theirs, how secure, how easy and how rich the loot! . . .

The greatest single hold of "the interests" is the fact that they are the "campaign contributors"—the men who supply the money for "keeping the party together," and for "getting out the vote." Did you ever think where the millions for watchers, spellbinders, halls, processions, posters, pamphlets, that are spent in national, state and local campaigns come from? Who pays the big election expenses of your congressman, of the men you send to the legislature to elect senators? Do you imagine those who foot those huge bills are fools? Don't you know that they make sure of getting their money back, with interest, compound upon compound? Your candidates get most of the money for their campaigns from the party committees; and the central party committee is the national committee with which congressional and state and local committees are affiliated. The bulk of the money for the "political trust" comes from "the interests." "The interests" will give only to the "political trust." And that means Aldrich and his Democratic (!) lieutenant, Gorman of Maryland, leader of the minority in the Senate. Aldrich, then, is the head of the "political trust" and Gorman is his right-hand man. When you speak of the Republican party, of the Democratic party, of the "good of the party," of the "best interests of the party," of "wise party policy," you mean what Aldrich and Gorman, acting for their clients, deem wise and proper and "Republican" or "Democratic." . . .

No railway legislation that was not either helpful to or harmless against "the interests"; no legislation on the subject of corporations that would interfere with "the interests," which use the corporate form to simplify and systematize their stealing; no legislation on the tariff question unless it secured to "the interests" full and free license to loot; no investigations of wholesale robbery or of any of the evils resulting from it—there you have in a few words the whole story of the Senate's treason under Aldrich's leadership, and of why property is concentrating in the hands of the few and the little children of the masses are being sent to toil in the darkness of mines, in the dreariness and unhealthfulness of factories instead of being sent to school; and why the great middle class—the old-fashioned Americans, the people with the incomes of from two thousand to fifteen thousand a year—is being swiftly crushed into dependence and the repulsive miseries of "genteel poverty." The heavy and ever heavier taxes of "the interests" are swelling rents, swelling the prices of food, clothing, fuel, all the necessities and all the necessary comforts. And the Senate both forbids the lifting of those taxes and levies fresh taxes for its master. . . .

Aldrich's real work—getting the wishes of his principals, directly or through their lawyers, and putting these wishes into proper form if they are orders for legislation or into the proper channels if they are orders to kill or emasculate legislation—this work is all done, of course, behind the scenes. When Aldrich is getting orders, there is of course never any witness. The second part of his task—execution—is in part a matter of whispering with his chief lieutenants, in part a matter of consultation in the secure secrecy of the Senate committee rooms. Aldrich is in person chairman of the chief Senate committee—finance. There he labors, assisted by Gorman, his right bower, who takes his place as chairman when the Democrats are in power; by Spooner, his left bower and public mouthpiece; by Allison, that Nestor of craft; by the Pennsylvania Railroad's Penrose; by Tom Platt of New York, corruptionist and lifelong agent of corruptionists; by Joe Bailey of Texas, and several other sympathetic or silent spirits. Together they concoct and sugar-coat the bitter doses for the people—the loot measures and the suffocating of the measures in restraint of loot. In the unofficial but powerful steering committee—which receives from him the will of "the interests" and translates it into "party policy"—he works through Allison as chairman —but Allison's position is recognized as purely honorary.

And, also, Aldrich sits in the powerful interstate-commerce committee; there, he has his "pal," the brazen Elkins of West Virginia, as chairman. He is not on the committee on appropriations; but Allison is, is its chairman, and Cullom of Illinois is there—and in due time we shall endeavor to get better acquainted with both of them. In the commerce committee, he has Frye of Maine, to look after such matters as the projected, often postponed, but never abandoned, loot through ship subsidy; in the Pacific Railroad committee he has the valiant soldier, the honest lumber and railway multi-millionaire, the embalmed-beef hero, Alger, as chairman; in the post-office and post-roads committee, which looks after the railways' postal graft, a clean steal from the Treasury of upward of ten millions a year—some put it as high as thirty millions—he has Penrose as chairman. In that highly important committee, the one on rules, he himself sits; but mouthpiece Spooner is naturally chairman. Their associates are Elkins and Lodge—another pair that need to be better known to the American people. Bailey is the chief "Democratic" member. What a sardonic jest to speak of these men as Republicans and Democrats!

READING NO. 17

Theodore Roosevelt Coins the Name "Muckraking" *

President Roosevelt disliked Phillips' attack on Senator Chauncey Depew and feared that the magazine writers were giving an unbalanced picture and stirring up popular unrest. When he used the term "muck-rake" at the annual off-the-record dinner of the Washington newspapermen, the response was favorable, and so the President repeated it in public at the corner-stone laying of the new House of Representatives Office Building. As was his pattern, Roosevelt used the occasion to lambast both the right and the left, attacking the corruptionists as well as their critics.

Over a century ago Washington laid the corner-stone of the Capitol in what was then little more than a tract of wooded wilderness here beside the Potomac. We now find it necessary to provide by great additional

* Theodore Roosevelt, Address at the laying of the corner-stone of the office building of the House of Representatives, April 14, 1906, from *The Works of Theodore Roosevelt*, XVI, Hermann Hagedorn, ed. (New York, 1926), pp. 415–424.

buildings for the business of the government. This growth in the need for the housing of the government is but a proof and example of the way in which the nation has grown and the sphere of action of the National Government has grown. We now administer the affairs of a nation in which the extraordinary growth of population has been outstripped by the growth of wealth and the growth in complex interests. The material problems that face us to-day are not such as they were in Washington's time, but the underlying facts of human nature are the same now as they were then. Under altered external form we war with the same tendencies toward evil that were evident in Washington's time, and are helped by the same tendencies for good. It is about some of these that I wish to say a word to-day.

In Bunyan's "Pilgrim's Progress" you may recall the description of the Man with the Muck-rake, the man who could look no way but downward, with the muck-rake in his hand; who was offered a celestial crown for his muck-rake, but who would neither look up nor regard the crown he was offered, but continued to rake to himself the filth of the floor.

In "Pilgrim's Progress" the Man with the Muck-rake is set forth as the example of him whose vision is fixed on carnal instead of on spiritual things. Yet he also typifies the man who in this life consistently refuses to see aught that is lofty, and fixes his eyes with solemn intentness only on that which is vile and debasing. Now, it is very necessary that we should not flinch from seeing what is vile and debasing. There is filth on the floor, and it must be scraped up with the muck-rake; and there are times and places where this service is the most needed of all the services that can be performed. But the man who never does anything else, who never thinks or speaks or writes, save of his feats with the muck-rake, speedily becomes, not a help to society, not an incitement to good, but one of the most potent forces for evil.

There are, in the body politic, economic and social, many and grave evils, and there is urgent necessity for the sternest war upon them. There should be relentless exposure of and attack upon every evil man whether politician or business man, every evil practice, whether in politics, in business, or in social life. I hail as a benefactor every writer or speaker, every man who, on the platform, or in book, magazine, or newspaper, with merciless severity makes such attack, provided always that he in his turn remembers that the attack is of use only if it is absolutely truthful. The liar is no whit better than the thief, and if his mendacity takes the form of slander, he may be worse than most thieves. It puts a premium upon knavery untruthfully to attack an honest man, or even with hysterical exaggeration to assail a bad man with untruth. An epidemic of indiscriminate assault upon character does not good, but very great harm. The soul of every scoundrel is gladdened whenever an honest man is assailed, or even when a scoundrel is untruthfully assailed. . . .

Any excess is almost sure to invite a reaction; and, unfortunately, the reaction, instead of taking the form of punishment of those guilty of the excess, is very apt to take the form either of punishment of the un-offending or of giving immunity, and even strength, to offenders. The effort to make financial or political profit out of the destruction of character can only result in public calamity. Gross and reckless assaults on character, whether on the stump or in newspaper, magazine, or book, create a morbid and vicious public sentiment, and at the same time act as a profound deterrent to able men of normal sensitiveness and tend to prevent them from entering the public service at any price. As an instance in point, I may mention that one serious difficulty encountered in getting the right type of men to dig the Panama Canal is the certainty that they will be exposed, both without, and, I am sorry to say, sometimes within, Congress, to utterly reckless assaults on their character and capacity.

At the risk of repetition let me say again that my plea is, not for immunity to but for the most unsparing exposure of the politician who betrays his trust, of the big business man who makes or spends his fortune in illegitimate or corrupt ways. There should be a resolute effort to hunt every such man out of the position he has disgraced. Expose the crime, and hunt down the criminal; but remember that even in the case of crime, if it is attacked in sensational, lurid, and untruthful fashion, the attack may do more damage to the public mind than the crime itself. It is because I feel that there should be no rest in the endless war against the forces of evil that I ask that the war be conducted with sanity as well as with resolution. The men with the muck-rakes are often indispensable to the well-being of society; but only if they know when to stop raking the muck, and to look upward to the celestial crown above them, to the crown of worthy endeavor. There are beautiful things above and roundabout them; and if they gradually grow to feel that the whole world is nothing but muck, their power of usefulness is gone. If the whole picture is painted black there remains no hue whereby to single out the rascals for distinction from their fellows. Such painting finally induces a kind of moral color-blindness; and people affected by it come to the conclusion that no man is really black, and no man really white, but they are all gray. In other words, they neither believe in the truth of the attack, nor in the honesty of the man who is attacked; they grow as suspicious of the accusation as of the offense; it becomes well-nigh hopeless to stir them either to wrath against wrong-doing or to enthusiasm for what is right; and such a mental attitude in the public gives hope to every knave, and is the despair of honest men. . . .

At this moment we are passing through a period of great unrest—social, political, and industrial unrest. It is of the utmost importance for our future that this should prove to be not the unrest of mere rebelliousness against life, of mere dissatisfaction with the inevitable inequality of conditions, but the unrest of a resolute and eager ambition to secure the betterment of the individual and the nation. So far as this movement of agitation throughout the country takes the form of a fierce discontent with evil, of a determination to punish the authors of evil, whether in industry or politics, the feeling is to be heartily welcomed as a sign of healthy life.

If, on the other hand, it turns into a mere crusade of appetite against appetite, of a contest between the brutal greed of the "have-nots" and the brutal greed of the "haves," then it has no significance for good, but only for evil. If it seeks to establish a line of cleavage, not along the line which divides good men from bad, but along that other line, running at right angles thereto, which divides those who are well off from those who are less well off, then it will be fraught with immeasurable harm to the body politic.

We can no more and no less afford to condone evil in the man of capital than evil in the man of no capital. The wealthy man who exults because there is a failure of justice in the effort to bring some trust magnate to an account for his misdeeds is as bad as, and no worse than, the so-called labor leader who clamorously strives to excite a foul class feeling on behalf of some other labor leader who is implicated in murder. One attitude is as bad as the other, and no worse; in each case the accused is entitled to exact justice; and in neither case is there need of action by others which can be construed into an expression of sympathy for crime.

It is a prime necessity that if the present unrest is to result in permanent good the emotion shall be translated into action, and that the action shall be marked by honesty, sanity, and self-restraint. There is mighty little good in a mere spasm of reform. The reform that counts is that which comes through steady, continuous growth; violent emotionalism leads to exhaustion.

It is important to this people to grapple with the problems connected with the amassing of enormous fortunes, and the use of those fortunes, both corporate and individual, in business. We should discriminate in the sharpest way between fortunes well-won and fortunes ill-won; between those gained as an incident to performing great services to the community as a whole, and those gained in evil fashion by keeping just within the limits of mere law-honesty. Of course no amount of charity in spending such fortunes in any way compensates for misconduct in making them. As a matter of personal conviction, and without pretending to discuss the details or formulate the system, I feel that we shall ultimately have to consider the adoption of some such scheme as that of a progressive tax on all fortunes, beyond a certain amount either given in life or devised or bequeathed upon death to any individual—a tax so framed as to put it out of the power of the owner of one of these enormous fortunes to hand on more than a certain amount to any one individual; the tax, of course, to be imposed by the National and not the State Government. Such taxation should, of course, be aimed merely at the inheritance or transmission in their entirety of those fortunes swollen beyond all healthy limits.

Again, the National Government must in some form exercise supervision over corporations engaged in interstate business—and all large corporations are engaged in interstate business—whether by license or otherwise, so as to permit us to deal with the far-reaching evils of overcapitalization. This year we are making a beginning in the direction of serious effort to settle some of these economic problems by the railway-rate legislation. Such legislation, if so framed, as I am sure it will be, as to secure definite and tangible results, will amount to something of itself; and it will amount to a great deal more in so far as it is taken as a first step in the direction of a policy of superintendence and control over corporate wealth engaged in interstate commerce, this superintendence and control not to be exercised in a spirit of malevolence toward the men who have created the wealth, but with the firm purpose both to do justice to them and to see that they in their turn do justice to the public at large.

The first requisite in the public servants who are to deal in this shape with corporations, whether as legislators or as executives, is honesty. This honesty can be no respecter of persons. There can be no such thing as unilateral honesty. The danger is not really from corrupt corporations; it springs from the corruption itself, whether exercised for or against corporations.

The eighth commandment reads: "Thou shalt not steal." It does not read: "Thou shalt not steal from the rich man." It does not read: "Thou shalt not steal from the poor man." It reads simply and plainly: "Thou shalt not steal." No good whatever will come from that warped and mock morality which denounces the misdeeds of men of wealth and forgets the misdeeds practised at their expense; which denounces bribery, but blinds itself to blackmail; which foams with rage if a corporation secures favors by improper methods, and merely leers with hideous mirth if the corporation is itself wronged. The only public servant who can be trusted honestly to protect the rights of the public against the misdeed of a corporation is that public man who will just as surely protect the corporation itself from wrongful aggression. If a public man is willing to yield to popular clamor and do wrong to the men of wealth or to rich corporations, it may be set down as certain that if the opportunity comes he will secretly and furtively do wrong to the public in the interest of a corporation. . . .

The men of wealth who to-day are trying to prevent the regulation and control of their business in the interest of the public by the proper government authorities will not succeed, in my judgment, in checking the progress of the movement. But if they did succeed they would find that they had sown the wind and would surely reap the whirlwind, for they would ultimately provoke the violent excesses which accompany a reform coming by convulsion instead of by steady and natural growth.

On the other hand, the wild preachers of unrest and discontent, the wild agitators against the entire existing order, the men who act crookedly, whether because of sinister design or from mere puzzle-head-edness, the men who preach destruction without proposing any substi-tute for what they intend to destroy, or who propose a substitute which would be far worse than the existing evils—all these men are the most dangerous opponents of real reform. If they get their way they will lead the people into a deeper pit than any into which they could fall under the present system. If they fail to get their way they will still do incalculable harm by provoking the kind of reaction which, in its revolt against the senseless evil of their teaching, would enthrone more securely than ever the very evils which their misguided followers believe they are attacking.

More important than aught else is the development of the broadest sympathy of man for man. The welfare of the wage-worker, the welfare of the tiller of the soil, upon these depend the welfare of the entire country; their good is not to be sought in pulling down others; but their good must be the prime object of all our statesmanship.

Materially we must strive to secure a broader economic opportunity for all men, so that each shall have a better chance to show the stuff of which he is made. Spiritually and ethically we must strive to bring about clean living and right thinking. We appreciate that the things of the body are important; but we appreciate also that the things of the soul are immeasurably more important. The foundation-stone of national life is and ever must be, the high individual character of the average citizen.

READING NO. **18**

The Pinchot-Ballinger Controversy*

A long-simmering conflict within the Taft Administration over the development of western lands came out in public when a young land office investigator was fired for opposing a grant of Alaskan coal lands. The conflict also led to the firing of Theodore Roosevelt's conservationist friend, Gifford Pinchot and a Congressional investigation that caught President Taft and Secretary of the Interior Ballinger lying. Collier's, in the middle of this first national environmental fight, published the story of the discharged investigator Louis Glavis, and used its cover as well as its contents to attack the Administration.

From 1902 to 1909 I was in the field service of the General Land Office, for the last two and a half years as Chief of Field Division. In September, 1909, I was summarily removed from my position without a formal hearing by Richard A. Ballinger, Secretary of the Interior, by authorization of the President of the United States. That removal was accompanied by the publication of a letter of the President to Mr. Ballinger. I believe that my removal was unfair. I believe the President's letter was grievously unfair, because in it the President gives weight to a charge against me which I never had the opportunity to see or answer. The President states in his letter that I withheld from him information favorable to my superiors. I do not know of any such information withheld by me, nor am I conscious of doing my superiors injustice. Nevertheless, I should not now make any public statement of the matter were it not still possible to save for the Government many thousands of acres of coal lands which I believe the Land Office may in the near future grant to fraudulent claimants. The hope that my statement will help to arouse public sentiment, and that this danger to the national resources may be averted, is what actuates me. This statement will

* Reading from Louis R. Glavis, "The Whitewashing of Ballinger," *Collier's*, XLIV (November 13, 1909), p. 15. Illustration from *Collier's*, XLIV (December 18, 1909), cover illustration.

simply give facts and leave to the judgment of those who read whether or not the Land Office has been zealous in the public service.

The coal lands of Alaska owned by the Government amount to over 100,000 acres. They are the future coal supply of the nation, of almost inestimable value. Possession of them by private individuals means great wealth—a monopoly by them would be a national menace.

On November 12, 1906, President Roosevelt withdrew all coal lands in Alaska from public entry; but previous to that time there were about 900 claims filed, covering about 100,000 acres (nearly the whole of the coal fields). The law attempts to prevent monopoly of such claims by limiting the amount of each claim and providing that each claimant must take up the land in his own interest and for his own use. This law has been interpreted by the Supreme Court of the United States to forbid speculating in coal lands before entry—either by dummy entrymen or by previous agreements to consolidate claims after entry. Of these 900 claims to Alaska coal lands—among them the so-called Cunningham group—the majority are fraudulent.

As to the action of the Land Office on these claims, I assert that the Land Office ordered the Cunningham claims to patent without due investigation when Commissioner Ballinger knew they were under suspicion; that while in office Commissioner Ballinger urged Congress to pass a law which would validate fraudulent Alaska claims; that shortly after resigning from office he became attorney for the Cunningham group and other Alaska claims; that soon after he became Secretary of the Interior his office rendered a decision which would have validated all fraudulent Alaska claims. A reversal of that decision on every point was obtained from Attorney-General Wickersham. Had it not been for Mr. Wickersham's decision, every fraudulent Alaska claim would have gone to patent. I assert that in the spring of 1909 the Land Office urged me to an early trial of these cases before the investigation was finished, and when Secretary Ballinger, as the President has stated, knew that the Cunningham claims were invalid. When I appealed to Secretary Ballinger for postponement, he referred me to his subordinates. The department of Agriculture intervened. I was superseded in the charge of the cases, and the man who superseded me endorsed my recommendations, and the postponement was granted. Immediately thereafter I made my report on the Cunningham cases to President Taft, and was dismissed from the service for insubordination.

READING NO. 19

Edwin Markham and the Struggle Against Child Labor*

As the journalists developed their analysis of twentieth-century industrial American life, some of them focused on the social conditions that underlay political corruption and economic concentration. They wrote about the

* Edwin Markham, "The Hoe-Man in the Making," *Cosmopolitan*, 41 (September, 1906), pp. 480–484.

workers, particularly the women and children in the sweat-shops, mines, and textile mills. The most famous depiction of the conditions of child labor was the series that Edwin Markham wrote in Cosmopolitan *in 1906–1907.*

Once, so the story goes, an old Indian chieftain was shown the ways and wonders of New York. He saw the cathedrals, the skyscrapers, the bleak tenements, the blaring mansions, the crowded circus, the airy span of Brooklyn Bridge. "What is the most surprising thing you have seen?" asked several comfortable Christian gentlemen of this benighted pagan whose worship was a "bowing down to stocks and stones." The savage shifted his red blanket, and answered in three slow words, "Little children working."

It has remained, then, for civilization to give the world an abominable custom which shocks the social ethics of even an unregenerate savage. For the Indian father does not ask his children to work, but leaves them free until the age of maturity, when they are ushered with solemn rites into the obligations of their elders. Some of us are wondering why our savage friends do not send their medicine men as missionaries, to shed upon our Christian darkness the light of barbarism. . . .

In the Southern cotton mills, where the doors shut out the odor of the magnolia and shut in the reeking damps and clouds of lint, and where the mocking bird outside keeps obbligato to the whirring wheels within, we find a gaunt goblin army of children keeping their forced march on the factory-floors—an army that out-watches the sun by day and the stars by night. Eighty thousand children, mostly girls, are at work in the textile mills of the United States. The South, the center of the cotton industry, happens to have the bad eminence of being the leader in this social infamy. At the beginning of 1903 there were in the South twenty thousand children at the spindles. The "Tradesman," of Chattanooga, estimates that with the springing up of new mills there must now be fifty thousand children at the Southern looms. This is thirty per cent. of all the cotton workers of the South—a spectral army of pigmy people sucked in from the hills to dance beside the crazing wheels.

Let us again reckon up this Devil's toll. In the North (where, God knows, conditions are bad enough), for every one thousand workers over sixteen years of age there are eighty-three workers under sixteen (that young old-age of the working-child); while in the South, for every one thousand workers in the mills over sixteen years of age there are three hundred and fifty-three under sixteen. Some of these are eight and nine years old, and some are only five and six. For a day or a night at a stretch these little children do some one monotonous thing—abusing their eyes in watching the rushing threads; dwarfing their muscles in an eternity of petty movements; befouling their lungs by breathing flecks of flying cotton; bestowing ceaseless, anxious attention for hours, where science says that "a twenty-minute strain is long enough for a growing mind." And these are not the children of recent immigrants, hardened by the effete conditions of foreign servitude. Nor are they negro children who have shifted their shackles from field to mill. They are white children of old and pure colonial stock. Think of it! Here is a people that has out-lived the bondage of England, that has seen the rise and fall of slavery—a people that must now fling their children into the clutches of capital, into the maw of the blind machine; must see their latest-born drag on in a base servility that reminds us of the Saxon churl under the frown of the Norman lord. For Mammon is merciless.

Fifty thousand children, mostly girls, are in the textile mills of the South. Six times as many children are working now as were working twenty years ago. Unless the conscience of the nation can be awakened, it will not be long before one hundred thousand children will be hobbling in hopeless lock-step to these Bastilles of labor. It will not be long till these little spinners shall be "far on the way to be spiders and needles."

Think of the deadly drudgery in these cotton mills. Children rise at half-past four, commanded by the ogre scream of the factory whistle; they hurry, ill fed, unkempt, unwashed, half dressed, to the walls which shut out the day and which confine them amid the din and dust and merciless maze of the machines. Here, penned in little narrow lanes, they look and leap and reach and tie among acres and acres of looms. Always the snow of the lint in their faces, always the thunder of the machines in their ears. A scant half-hour at noon breaks the twelve-hour vigil, for it is nightfall when the long hours end and the children may return to the barracks they call "home," often too tired to wait for the cheerless meal which the mother, also working in the factory, must cook, after her factory-day is over. Frequently at noon and at night they fall asleep with the food unswallowed in the mouth. Frequently they snatch only a bite and curl up undressed on the bed, to gather strength for the same dull round to-morrow, and to-morrow, and to-morrow.

When I was in the South I was everywhere charmed by the bright courtesy of the cultured classes, but I was everywhere depressed by the stark penury of the working-people. This penury stands grimly out in the gray monotonous shells that they call "homes"—dingy shacks, or bleak, barn-like structures. And for these dirty, desolate homes the workers must pay rent to the mill-owner. But the rent is graded according to the number of children sent to work in the mill. The more the children, the less the rent. Mammon is wise: he knows how to keep a cruel grip upon the tots at the fireside.

And why do these children know no rest, no play, no learning, nothing but the grim grind of existence? Is it because we are all naked and shivering? Is it because there is sudden destitution in the land? Is it because pestilence walks at noonday? Is it because war's red hand is pillaging our storehouses and burning our cities? No, forsooth! Never before were the storehouses so crammed to bursting with bolts and bales of every warp and woof. No, forsooth! The children, while yet in the gristle, are ground down that a few more useless millions may be heaped up. We boast that we are leading the commercialism of the world, and we grind in our mills the bones of the little ones to make good our boast.

Rev. Edgar Murphy of Montgomery, Alabama, has photographed many groups of these pathetic little toilers, all under twelve. Jane Addams saw in a night-factory a little girl of five, her teeth blacked with snuff, like all the little ones about her—a little girl who was busily and clumsily tying threads in coarse muslin. The average child lives only four years after it enters the mills. Pneumonia stalks in the damp, lint-filled rooms, and leads hundreds of the little ones out to rest. Hundreds more are maimed by the machinery, two or three for each of their elders. One old millhand carries sixty-four scars, the cruel record of the shuttles.

The labor commissioner of North Carolina reports that there are two hundred and sixty-one cotton mills in that state, in which nearly forty thousand people are employed, including nearly eight thousand children. The average daily wage of the men is fifty-seven cents, of the women thirty-nine cents, of the children twenty-two cents. The commissioner goes on to say: "I have talked with a little boy of seven years who worked for forty nights in Alabama, and with another child who, at six years of age, had been on the night-shift eleven months. Little boys turned out at two o'clock in the morning, afraid to go home, would beg a clerk in the mill for permission to lie down on the office floor. In one city mill in the South, a doctor said he had amputated the fingers of more than one hundred children, mangled in the mill machinery, and that a horrible form of dropsy occurs frequently among the overworked children."

Irene Macfadyen of England, after inspecting our conditions, a year or two ago, wrote: "The physical, mental, and moral effect of these long hours of toil on the children is indescribably sad. Mill children are so stunted that every foreman will tell you that you cannot judge their ages. The lint in their lungs forms a perfect cultivating medium for tuberculosis and pneumonia, and consumption is common among them. Many die after a few years of this service." The "Washington Post," commenting on child-labor in the South, says: "The average life of the children after they go into the mills is four years. It would be less cruel for a state to have children painlessly put to death than it is to permit them to be ground to death by this awful process."

READING NO. 20

Ben Lindsey, The Kid's Judge*

The conditions under which children labored in the factories and lived in the slums produced movements to ban child labor and to set up a juvenile court system. The membership overlapped, and the enemy of both often turned out to be business power and greed. Judge Ben Lindsey of Colorado became a genuine hero of both movements and found that trying to improve the lot of the children brought him up against most of the major economic and political interests of his state.

Of course, he didn't realize at first what he was warring against. Brought up in a perfectly conventional way, his notions of life and economics were perfectly commonplace; but when men came to him and in the name of "business," "the party," and "property" besought him not to fight so hard for the children, he began to see that the enemy of men, as of children, was not men, but things. Once he and a police captain had a dispute in chambers over the custody of some boys arrested for stealing bicycles. The police wanted to hold the boys. Why? The Judge couldn't make out till the officers said something about the owners of the wheels wanting to "get back their property."

"Oh," said the Judge, "I see the difference between you and me: you want to recover the property, while I want to recover the boys."

The Judge recovered both.

A cotton mill was set up in Colorado. That was a new industry, and the men who established it were applauded for their "enterprise, which could not but benefit the whole State." To compete with the South, however, this mill had to employ child labour. The kids' Judge heard that they were importing large families and setting the little children to work. Colorado had a child-labour law, and the Judge went to the mill to see if the law was being violated. It was, and the conditions were pitiful.

"These imported people were practically slaves," he says. "They had

* Lincoln Steffens, "Ben Lindsey, The Just Judge," reprinted in *Upbuilders* (New York, 1909), pp. 202–205.

come out under contracts, and the children, unschooled, toiled at the machines first to liberate their parents, then to support them."

The Judge warned the milling company, but that did no good, so he had criminal proceedings instituted, and not only against the superintendent, but against the higher officers also.

This is not the custom in the United States, and the president of the mill, who was also one of the big men in the Colorado Fuel & Iron Company, called on the Judge to explain that he was a respectable citizen. The Judge suggested that it wasn't proper to try to influence a judge in a pending case, but the president "didn't want to do anything improper"; all he wanted was to remind the Judge that a conviction in the case would make him (the president) a criminal. "And I am no criminal," he said. The Judge replied that he was if he broke the law. But the president didn't break the law. If the law was broken, it was by his superintendent, and it was all right to fine his superintendent. But the president was a gentleman and a "big man."

"I'd rather fine you than your superintendent," said the Judge. "He is only your agent, and, as you intimate, you wouldn't mind if he were punished. So I'll punish you as I warned you; I told you that if he persisted in violating the law for you, I'd hold you responsible."

"But, Judge," he said, "if you are going to keep up this fight, we will close the mill!" And he proceeded to tell what a great industry it was; how many people it gave employment; how much good it was doing to the city (he meant the business) of Denver; and how much money had been invested in it by himself and other capitalists.

"His point of view," the Judge says, "was perfectly plain. Money was sacred, men were of no account. If business went well, children could go to—well, let us say, to work. And he blamed me, not the Law, not the State; he had no fear of these. I, personally, with my queer regard for men and women and children—I was a menace to business."

"I warn you right now," he said to the Judge, "that if this thing keeps up, we will shut down the mill, and you will have to share the consequences."

And Judge Lindsey replied: "We are here to protect the children and to enforce the Law, and all I regret is that the penalty isn't imprisonment instead of a fine, so that I could be sure of preventing you from employing young children."

And the Judge persisted, and the mill was closed down. Other causes contributed, but Lindsey never shirked his "share of the responsibility."

What is more, Judge Lindsey had the child-labour law made stricter. He can put "money" in prison now if it hurts children. He had to fight business and politics and the police to do it, but he did it; he and the kids and the men and women of Denver.

READING NO. 21

George Kibbe Turner and The
Daughters of the Poor*

Once the movement got well started, most of the muckrakers came to tie poverty and exploitive social conditions to machine politics and big business. G. K. Turner, who replaced Lincoln Steffens as McClure's *municipal expert, was not convinced of the big business contribution, but he gained considerable recognition for his studies of the relationships between prostitution, the saloon, and politics.*

THE DAUGHTERS OF THE POOR

A PLAIN STORY OF THE DEVELOPMENT OF NEW YORK CITY AS A LEADING CENTER OF THE WHITE SLAVE TRADE OF THE WORLD, UNDER TAMMANY HALL

There are now three principal centers of the so-called white slave trade—that is, the recruiting and sale of young girls of the poorer classes by procurers. The first is the group of cities in Austrian and Russian Poland, headed by Lemberg; the second is Paris; and the third the city of New York. In the past ten years New York has become the leader of the world in this class of enterprise. The men engaged in it there have taken or shipped girls, largely obtained from the tenement districts of New York, to every continent on the globe; they are now doing business with Central and South America, Africa, and Asia. They are driving all competitors before them in North America. And they have established, directly or indirectly, recruiting systems in every large city of the United States.

The story of the introduction of this European business into New

* George Kibbe Turner, "The Daughters of the Poor," *McClure's*, 34 (November, 1909), pp. 45, 58–59.

York, under the protection of the Tammany Hall political organization, its extension from there through the United States, and its shipments of women to the four corners of the earth, is a strange one; it would seem incredible if it were not thoroughly substantiated by the records of recent municipal exposures in half a dozen great American cities, by two independent investigations by the United States Government during the past year, and by the common knowledge of the people of the East Side tenement district of New York, whose daughters and friends' daughters have been chiefly exploited by it. . . .

During the past six or seven years the police of most large American cities outside of New York have noticed a strange development which they have never been able to explain entirely to themselves. The business enterprises for marketing girls have passed almost entirely from the hands of women into those of men. In every case these men have the most intimate connections with the political machines of the slums, and everywhere there has developed a system of local cadets.

The date of this new development of the white slave trade outside of New York corresponds almost uniformly with the time when the traders and cadets from the New York redlight district introduced New York methods into the other cities of the country in 1901 and 1902. Hundreds of New York dealers and cadets are still at work in these other cities. But much more important are the local youths, whom these missionaries of the devil brought by the sight of their sleek prosperity into their trade. Everywhere the boy of the slums has learned that a girl is an asset which, once acquired by him, will give him more money than he can ever earn, and a life of absolute ease. In Chicago, for example, prosecutions in 1908 conducted by Assistant State's Attorney Clifford G. Roe caused to be fined or sent to prison one hundred and fifty of these cadets, nearly all local boys, who had procured local working-girls from the dance-halls and cheap pleasure resorts in and around Chicago.

THE DOUBLE INFLUENCE OF THE NEW SYSTEM

There is little doubt that from now on the larger part of the procuring and marketing of women for the United States will be carried on by the system of political procurers developed in New York. The operation of this system has a double influence upon our large cities. On the one side, it has great political importance, for the reason that more and more, with the growing concentration of the slum politician upon this field, the procurer and marketer of women tends to hold the balance of power in city elections. This is true not alone in New York; analyzers of recent political contests in Philadelphia and Chicago have been convinced that the registration and casting of fraudulent votes from disorderly places in those cities may easily determine the result in a close city election, for false votes by the thousand are cast from these resorts.

Certainly this is not an over-scrupulous class to hold the balance of political power in a community. But it is the other influence of the development that counts most—its highly efficient system for procuring its supplies. The average life of women in this trade is not over five years, and supplies must be constantly replenished. There is something appalling in the fact that year after year the demands of American cities reach up through thousands to the tens of thousands for new young girls. The supply has come in the past and must come in the future from the girls morally broken by the cruel social pressure of poverty and lack of training. The odds have been enough against these girls in the past. Now everywhere through the great cities of the country the sharp eyes of the wise cadet are watching, hunting her out at her amusements and places of work. And back of him the most adroit minds of the politicians of the slums are standing to protect and extend with him their mutual interests.

The trade of procuring and selling girls in America—taken from the weak hands of women and placed in control of acute and greedy men—has organized and specialized after its kind exactly as all other business has done. The cadet does his procuring, not as an agent for any larger interest, but knowing that a woman can always be sold profitably either on the streets or in houses in American cities. The larger operators conduct their houses and get their supplies from the cadet—take him, in fact, into a sort of partnership, by which every week he collects the girl's wages as her agent. The ward politician keeps the disorderly saloon—a most natural political development, because it serves both as a "hang-out" for the gangs of cadets and thieves, and a market for women. And, back of this, the politician higher up takes his share in other ways. No business pays such toll to the slum politicians as this does. The First Ward ball of "Hincky Dink" Kenna and "Bath House John" Coughlin, the kings of slum politics in Chicago; the Larry Mulligan ball in New York; the dances of the Kelly and East Side and Five Points New York gangs, all draw their chief revenue, directly or indirectly, from this source. From low to high, the whole strong organization gorges and fattens on the gross feeding from this particular thing.

READING NO. 22

Ray Stannard Baker's Following the Color Line*

Ray Stannard Baker went south to write an account of "the great Atlanta race riot" of 1906. The response to his story was good, and Baker proceeded to spend two years researching race relations in the North and South. He described the rising racial antagonism as well as a growing unwillingness of the black "underman" to "keep his place" at the bottom of an American caste system.

It keeps coming to me that this is more a white man's problem than it is a Negro problem. The white man as well as the black is being tried by fire. The white man is in full control of the South, politically, socially, industrially: the Negro, as ex-Governor Northen points out, is his helpless ward. What will he do with him? Speaking of the education of the Negro, and in direct reference to the conditions in Atlanta which I have already described, many men have said to me:

"Think of the large sums that the South has spent and is spending on the education of the Negro. The Negro does not begin to pay for his education in taxes."

Neither do the swarming Slavs, Italians, and Poles in our Northern cities. They pay little in taxes and yet enormous sums are expended in their improvement. For their benefit? Of course, but chiefly for ours. It is better to educate men in school than to let them so educate themselves as to become a menace to society. The present *kind* of education in the South may possibly be wrong; but for the protection of society it is as necessary to train every Negro as it is every white man.

When I saw the crowds of young Negroes being made criminal— through lack of proper training—I could not help thinking how pitilessly ignorance finally revenges itself upon that society which neglects or exploits it. . . .

* Reprinted as Ray Stannard Baker, *Following the Color Line* (New York, 1908), pp. 65, 118–119, 123–124, 131–132, 296–297.

In Boston, of all places, I expected to find much of the old sentiment. It does exist among some of the older men and women, but I was surprised at the general attitude which I encountered. It was one of hesitation and withdrawal. Summed up, I think the feeling of the better class of people in Boston (and elsewhere in Northern cities) might be thus stated:

We have helped the Negro to liberty; we have helped to educate him; we have encouraged him to stand on his own feet. Now let's see what he can do for himself. After all, he must survive or perish by his own efforts.

In short, they have "cast the bantling on the rocks."

Though they still preserve the form of encouraging the Negro, the spirit seems to have fled. Not long ago the Negroes of Boston organised a concert at which Theodore Drury, a coloured musician of really notable accomplishments, was to appear. Aristocratic white people were appealed to and bought a considerable number of tickets; but on the evening of the concert the large block of seats purchased by white people was conspicuously vacant. Northern white people would seem to be more interested in the distant Southern Negro than in the Negro at their doors.

Before I take up the cruder and more violent expressions of prejudice on the part of the lower class of white men in the North I want to show the beginnings of cold-shouldering as it exists in varying degrees in Northern cities, and especially in Boston, the old centre of abolitionism.

Superficially, at least, the Negro in Boston still enjoys the widest freedom; but after one gets down to real conditions he finds much complaint and alarm on the part of Negroes over growing restrictions. . . .

Even at Harvard where the Negro has always enjoyed exceptional opportunities, conditions are undergoing a marked change. A few years ago a large class of white students voluntarily chose a brilliant Negro student, R. C. Bruce, as valedictorian. But last year a Negro baseball player was the cause of so much discussion and embarrassment to the athletic association that there will probably never be another coloured boy on the university teams. The line has already been drawn, indeed, in the medical department. Although a coloured doctor only a few years ago was house physician at the Boston Lying-in-Hospital, coloured students are no longer admitted to that institution. One of them, Dr. Welker (an Iowa coloured man), cannot secure his degree because he hasn't had six obstetrical cases, and he can't get the six cases because he isn't admitted with his white classmates to the Lying-in-Hospital. It is a curious fact that not only the white patients but some Negro patients object to the coloured doctors. In a recent address which has awakened much sharp comment among Boston Negroes, President Eliot of

Harvard indicated his sympathy with the general policy of separate education in the South by remarking that if Negro students were in the majority at Harvard, or formed a large proportion of the total number, some separation of the races might follow. . . .

As I travelled in the North, I heard many stories of the difficulties which the coloured man had to meet in getting employment. Of course, as a Negro said to me, "there are always places for the coloured man at the bottom." He can always get work at unskilled manual labour, or personal or domestic service—in other words, at menial employment. He has had that in plenty in the South. But what he seeks as he becomes educated is an opportunity for better grades of employment. He wants to rise.

It is not, then, his complaint that he cannot get work in the North, but that he is limited in his opportunities to rise, to get positions which his capabilities (if it were not for his colour) would entitle him to. He is looking for a place where he will be judged at his worth as a man, not as a Negro: this he came to the North to find, and he meets difficulties of which he had not dreamed in the South.

At Indianapolis I found a great discussion going on over what to do with the large number of idle young coloured people, some of whom had been through the public schools, but who could not, apparently, find any work to do. As an able coloured man said to me: "What shall we do? Here are our young people educated in the schools, capable of doing good work in many occupations where skill and intelligence are required—and yet with few opportunities opening for them. They don't want to dig ditches or become porters or valets any more than intelligent white boys; they are human. The result is that some of them drop back into idle discouragement—or worse." . . .

A decided tendency also exists to charge up to the Negro, because he is a Negro, all the crimes which are commonly committed by any ignorant, neglected, poverty-stricken people. Only last summer we had in New York what the newspaper reporters called a "crime wave." The crime in that case was what is designated in the South as the "usual crime" (offences against women) for which Negroes are lynched. But in New York not a Negro was implicated.

I was struck while in Philadelphia by a presentment of a grand jury in Judge Kinsey's court upon the subject of a "crime wave" which read thus:

> In closing our duties as jurymen, we wish to call to the attention of this court the large proportion of cases presented to us for action wherein the offences were charged to either persons of foreign birth or those of the coloured race, and we feel that some measures should be

taken to the end that our city should be relieved of both the burden of the undesirable alien and the irresponsible coloured person.

Here, it will be seen, the "undesirable alien" and "irresponsible coloured person" are classed together, although it is significant of the greater prejudice against the coloured man that the newspaper report of the action of the grand jury should be headed "Negro Crime Abnormal," without referring to the alien at all. When I inquired at the prosecutor's office about the presentment, I was told:

"Oh, the dagoes are just as bad as the Negroes."

And both are bad, not because they are Negroes or Italians, but because they are ignorant, neglected, poverty-stricken.

Thus in the dust and confusion of the vast readjustments now going on in the South, the discomfort of which both races feel but neither quite understands, we have the white man blindly blaming the Negro and the Negro blindly hating the white. When they both understand that many of the troubles they are having are only the common gall-spots of the new industrial harness there will be a better living together.

I do not wish to imply, of course, that an industrial age or the wage system furnishes an ideal condition for race relationships; for in the North the Negro's struggle for survival in the competitive field is accompanied, as I have shown elsewhere, by the severest suffering. The conditions of Negroes in Indianapolis, New York, and Philadelphia is in some ways worse than it is anywhere in the South. But, say what we will, the wage system is one step upward from the old feudalism. The Negro is treated less like a slave and more like a man in the North. It is for this reason that Negroes, no matter what their difficulties of making a living in the North, rarely wish to go back to the South. And as the South develops industrially it will approximate more nearly to Northern conditions. In Southern cities to-day, because of industrial development, the Negro is treated more like a man than he is in the country; and this is one reason why Negroes crowd into the cities and can rarely be persuaded to go back into the country—unless they can own their own land.

But the South is rapidly shaking off the remnants of the old feudalism. Development of mines and forests, the extension of manufacturing, the introduction of European immigrants, the inflow of white Northerners, better schools, more railroads and telephones, are all helping to bring the South up to the economic standard of the North. There will be a further breakup of baronial tenant farming, the plantation store will disappear, the ruinous credit system will be abolished, and there will be a widespread appearance of independent farm-owners, both white and black. This will all tend to remove the personal and sentimental attitude of the old Southern life; the Negro will of necessity be judged more and more as a man, not as a slave or dependent. In short, the country, South and North, will become economically more homogeneous.

But even when the South reaches the industrial development of the North the Negro problem will not be solved; it is certainly not solved in New York or Philadelphia, where industrial development has reached its highest form. The prejudice in those cities, as I have shown, has been growing more intense as Negro population increased. What, then, will happen?

READING NO. 23

The Failure of the Churches*

As they "muckraked" the rest of society, some of the journalists became aware that not only was organized religion's social message sadly inadequate, but also that the churches sometimes contributed directly to the social problems. Such was the case of New York City's wealthy, old Trinity Church, which had one of the largest slum landholdings in the city.

On the lower West Side of New York City, in the old Eighth Ward and not far from the docks, is a place called Hudson Park, where in certain poor piles of sand the little children of the tenements sometimes come to play.

It is not much of a park; a little slice of rescued city space, a mere glimpse of open sky, a part of a city block without the usual hideous city houses and set with weary trees, uncertain grass, some rigid benches—no more than that. In the center, a curious and unreasonable depression adorned with some doubtful classicism, and at the rear the sand piles where the chalk-faced children play. That is all.

And yet you, looking upon it, poor and forlorn as it is, feel in your heart an impulse to fall upon your knees there in the reek of the filthy street and utter gratitude for even so much. All about you to the south blink the frowsy, scaly, slatternly, bleary, decayed, and crumbling old

* Charles Edward Russell, "The Tenements of Trinity Church," *Everybody's*, XIX (July, 1908), p. 47.

houses, leering from dirty windows like old drunkards through blood-shot eyes; the broken shutters awry like deformities, the doors agape like old, toothless mouths. All about is the hell of the West Side tenement-house region, and compared with its outward and visible signs, this maidenhood of Hudson Park, albeit ill-clad and gawky, is something sweet. You think back upon the years of dreary struggle and contest and argument and travail that were required to secure this little island of sanity in the mad region around you, and wonder to yourself if we are all perfectly crazy that we tolerate such things.

Drunken, disreputable, decayed, topsy-turvy old houses, the homes of thousands of families and the breeding-places for so many children that are to carry on the world's work—who owns these terrible places? Who draws the wretched profit of their existence?

Trinity Church, holder of one of the greatest estates in New York or in the country, owns many of them. This is the heart of her possessions: street after street is lined with her properties. Here is Clarkson Street, on the south of the tiny park—she owns a dozen tenement properties there; Varick Street, crossing Clarkson at right angles—she owns sixty-six tenement properties there; West Houston, noisome and dilapidated—she owns fifty-one tenement properties there; upper Greenwich Street—she owns sixty-five tenement properties there; Charlton Street, a dreary place—she owns twenty-six tenement properties there; Canal Street toward the North River—she owns forty-seven tenement properties there; Hudson Street—she owns 138 tenement properties there. You do not think well of the appearance of Vandam Street; Trinity owns forty-one tenement properties there. You think Barrow Street down here looks ancient and seedy; Trinity owns twenty-two tenement properties there. Wherever you walk in this dreadful region, you find something that Trinity owns, and, as a rule, it is something that you know she ought not to own.

READING NO. 24

Will Irwin and The American Newspaper*

As professional journalists, the muckrakers were concerned about the state of the press. Many of them wrote about it, and in 1911 Will Irwin

* Will Irwin, "The American Newspaper, A Study of Journalism in Its Relation to the Public," *Collier's*, 47 (June 17, 1911), p. 18.

authored a fifteen article series on "The American Newspaper" for Collier's. In it he described the shift in the newspaper role from being the vehicle of its editors' opinions to that of an information disseminator. The greatest problem facing the newspapers in the twentieth century was that they had become great commercial enterprises, subject to almost irresistible pressure from advertisers, whose revenue they needed.

The American Tobacco Company has availed itself of this weakness in the press; and, more recently, the Sugar Trust. The late sugar exposé, in which Secretary of War Stimson won his spurs, came in two episodes—a little tempest, prematurely lulled, and then the storm. During the lull the Trust inserted in the newspaper trade journals advertisements and "reading notices," proclaiming a $100,000 advertising campaign in the newspapers, and communicated with publishers to the same effect. They never asked any favors—doubtless, like O'Day, they were too wise to take that risk. They must have known that the sight of such a large, profitable advertisement in his pages would influence a weak brother here and there, make him tone down his editorial attacks or withhold his hand altogether. A national advertising expert who has done such work sums it up as follows: "Advertising is practical psychology. I know that the advertisement is a kind of tacit offer of friendship. It won't silence all the press, nor even most of it, but I calculate that it will take at least twenty-five per cent of the force out of a general newspaper attack."

We have just witnessed, however, a case where the work must have been done not with a rapier but with a bludgeon. The Coca-Cola Company of Atlanta, maker of a popular soda-fountain beverage, has been through another phase of its litigation with the Government's pure-food experts. Dr. Harvey W. Wiley charged that the addition of free caffein to the mixture was in violation of law. The case was tried in Chattanooga, and the company won. Now Coca-Cola is one of the greatest of national advertisers, and it uses the newspapers liberally in the "dry" South, where its wares are widely consumed as a non-alcoholic substitute for liquor. Many Southern newspapers demanded that the Associated Press carry news of the trial. The Associated Press, being servant to the whole body of its newspapers, very properly acquiesced. So the decision was freely reported—even as far north as New York, where a Hearst paper carried the story. Not only that; hard upon the decision some Southern newspaper or other printed a leading editorial deploring "the attack on a great Southern industry." This editorial was clipped in full all through the Southern press, even in districts far too remote from Atlanta to be affected in the least by the success or failure of the Coca-Cola Company. A clipping of the editorial used to arrive in the newspaper offices in the same mail with the advance advertising copy of Coca-Cola. A word to the wise which was usually sufficient.

In the panic of 1907 and the curiously brief hard times which followed, the press of the United States generally published its idea of the exact truth about the situation in Wall Street far, far away, and kept still about the home situation, or lied. Certain managing editors present a vehement defense for this course. "The end justifies the means." They say that the depression was brief and harmless, as compared to the hard times of 1873 and 1893, just because the newspapers howled prosperity and hid the real conditions. This might stand as a defense, except for one fact. Newspapers which lied most brazenly were assuming to be tribunes of the "common people," and on the common people this policy often weighed most cruelly. Pittsburg was hard hit. Two banks had failed, mills were closing every day. The Pittsburg newspapers suddenly began printing "news" of a great industrial revival. So, thought the financial powers, people would spend their money instead of hoarding it, and business would go on. Well, it did go on, and Pittsburg recovered. But four thousand discharged mill-hands from outside cities read these false reports and crowded into Pittsburg, to find further poverty and misery.

Or again: the Chicago banks weathered the crisis well, yet many of them refused cash to depositors, issuing instead cashier's checks to pay running expenses. Why? They were getting from New York call loan rates on their money. This was oppression—taking advantage of distress to fill their pockets. The financial reporters all knew about this process. It was news—good news. Perhaps they turned the story into their offices; more likely they saved themselves the trouble. At any rate, none printed it.

In 1901, when bubonic plague first appeared in San Francisco, "big business" and the advertisers decided that the newspapers should be not only silent but false, lest tourists, settlers, and customers shun the city. The publishers met in the famous "midnight conference." All save the Hearst man pledged themselves to lie about the plague situation; and the Hearst man joined the majority before long. The Government experts found that the plague had arrived. The newspapers reviled them, hampered their work, rendered their quarantines ineffective. The plague lingered. San Francisco is only just finished with fighting it. Had the newspapers told the truth in 1901, they would have saved the city some lives, and millions of dollars. In this case no one directly threatened withdrawal of advertising; the fact that the financial powers, including the great department stores, were strongly on one side was enough for publishers and managing editors trained in the modern commercial school.

READING NO. 25

Walter Lippmann on the Meaning
of Muckraking*

*Walter Lippmann graduated from Harvard, became Lincoln Steffens'
research assistant on* Everybody's, *and went on from there to a brief stint as
private secretary to the new Socialist Mayor of Schenectady. In his 1914
analysis of Progressive Era values and change, he attempted to sum up the
meaning of muckraking. There was a growing recognition in the nation, he
argued, that the ethics of the commercial world were unsuited for public life.*

There is in America to-day a distinct prejudice in favor of those who
make the accusations. . . .

The sense of conspiracy and secret scheming which transpire is almost
uncanny. "Big Business," and its ruthless tentacles, have become the
material for the feverish fantasy of illiterate thousands thrown out of
kilter by the rack and strain of modern life. It is possible to work
yourself into a state where the world seems a conspiracy and your daily
going is beset with an alert and tingling sense of labyrinthine evil.
Everything askew—all the frictions of life are readily ascribed to a
deliberate evil intelligence, and men like Morgan and Rockefeller take
on attributes of omnipotence, that ten minutes of cold sanity would
reduce to a barbarous myth. I know a socialist who seriously believes
that the study of eugenics is a Wall Street scheme for sterilizing
working-class leaders. And the cartoons which pictured Morgan sitting
arrogantly in a chariot drawn by the American people in a harness of
ticker tape—these are not so much caricatures as pictures of what no
end of fairly sane people believe. Not once but twenty times have I been
told confidentially of a nation-wide scheme by financiers to suppress
every radical and progressive periodical. But even though the most
intelligent muckrakers have always insisted that the picture was absurd,

* Walter Lippmann, *Drift and Mastery* (New York, 1914), pp. 1–5,
10–16.

it remains to this day a very widespread belief. I remember how often Lincoln Steffens used to deplore the frightened literalness with which some of his articles were taken. One day in the country he and I were walking the railroad track. The ties, of course, are not well spaced for an ordinary stride, and I complained about it. "You see," said Mr. Steffens with mock obviousness, "Morgan controls the New Haven and he prefers to make the people ride."

Now it is not very illuminating to say that this smear of suspicion has been worked up by the muckrakers. If business and politics really served American need, you could never induce people to believe so many accusations against them. It is said, also, that the muckrakers played for circulation, as if that proved their insincerity. But the mere fact that muckraking was what people wanted to hear is in many ways the most important revelation of the whole campaign.

There is no other way of explaining the quick approval which the muckrakers won. They weren't voices crying in a wilderness, or lonely prophets who were stoned. They demanded a hearing; it was granted. They asked for belief; they were believed. They cried that something should be done and there was every appearance of action. There must have been real causes for dissatisfaction, or the land notorious for its worship of success would not have turned so savagely upon those who had achieved it. . . .

Now if you study the chief themes of muckraking I think it is possible to see the outlines of what America has come to expect.

The first wave of exposure insisted upon the dishonesty of politicians. Close upon it came widespread attack upon big business men, who were charged with bribing officials and ruining their competitors. Soon another theme appeared: big business men were accused of grafting upon the big corporations which they controlled. We are entering upon another period now: not alone big business, but all business and farming too, are being criticized for inefficiency, for poor product, and for exploitation of employees.

This classification is, of course, a very rough one. It would be easy enough to dispute it, for the details are endlessly complicated and the exceptions may appear very large to some people. But I think, nevertheless, that this classification does no essential violence to the facts. It doesn't matter for my purposes that some communities are still in what I call the first period, while others are in the third. For a nation like ours doesn't advance at the same rate everywhere. All I mean to suggest is that popular muckraking in the last decade has shifted its interest in something like this order: First, to the corruption of aldermen and mayors and public servants by the boss acting for a commercial interest, and to the business methods of those who built up the trusts.

Then, muckraking turned, and began to talk about the milking of railroads by banks, and of one corporation by another. This period laid great emphasis on the "interlocking directorate." Now, muckraking is fastening upon the waste in management, upon working conditions as in the Steel Mills or at Lawrence, or upon the quality of service rendered by the larger corporations. These have been the big themes. . . .

We can see, I think, what people meant by the word graft. They did not mean robbery. It is rather confused rhetoric to call a grafter a thief. His crime is not that he filches money from the safe but that he betrays a trust. The grafter is a man whose loyalty is divided and whose motives are mixed. A lawyer who takes a fee from both sides in some case; a public official who serves a private interest; a railroad director who is also a director in the supply company; a policeman in league with outlawed vice: those are the relationships which the American people denounce as "corrupt." The attempt to serve at the same time two antagonistic interests is what constitutes "corruption."

The crime is serious in proportion to the degree of loyalty that we expect. A President of the United States who showed himself too friendly to some private interest would be denounced, though he may not have made one cent out of the friendship. But where we have not yet come to expect much loyalty we do very little muckraking. So if you inquired into the ethics of the buyer in almost any manufacturing house, you would find him doing things daily that would land the purchasing agent of a city in jail. Who regards it as especially corrupt if the selling firm "treats" the buyer, gives him or her a "present," perhaps a commission, or at least a "good time"? American life is saturated with the very relationship which in politics we call corrupt. The demand for a rake-off . . . it saturates the work-a-day world with tips and fees and "putting you on to a good thing" and "letting you in on the ground floor." But in the politician it is mercilessly condemned.

That is because we expect more of the politician. We say in effect that no public servant must allow himself to follow the economic habits of his countrymen. The corrupt politician is he who brings into public service the traditions of a private career. Perhaps that is a cynical reflection. I do not know how to alter it. When I hear politicians talk "reform," I know they are advocating something which most drummers on the road would regard as the scruples of a prig, and I know that when business men in a smoking-room are frank, they are taking for granted acts which in a politician we should call criminal.

For the average American will condemn in an alderman what in his partner he would consider reason for opening a bottle of champagne. In literal truth the politician is attacked for displaying the morality of his constituents. You might if you didn't understand the current revolution, consider that hypocrisy. It isn't: it is one of the hopeful signs of the age. For it means that unconsciously men regard some of the interests of life as too important for the intrusion of commercial ethics.

Further Reading

The best general descriptions of the United States during the muckrake years are Mark Sullivan's popular *Our Times*, Vols. I–III (New York, 1926–1930) and George E. Mowry's scholarly *The Era of Theodore Roosevelt, 1900–1912* (New York, 1958). Helpful for interpreting the period are Loren P. Beth, *The Development of the American Constitution, 1877–1917* (New York, 1971), David M. Kennedy, ed., *Progressivism: The Critical Issues* (Boston, 1971), Otis L. Graham, Jr., *An Encore for Reform* (New York, 1967), and Robert H. Wiebe, *The Search for Order, 1877–1920* (New York, 1967).

William H. Harbaugh, *Power and Responsibility, The Life and Times of Theodore Roosevelt* (New York, 1961), ably explains Roosevelt's attitudes toward the Muckrakers, but there is no substitute for *The Letters of Theodore Roosevelt*, Vol. 5, edited by Elting Morison, John M. Blum, and Alfred D. Chandler, Jr. (Cambridge, Mass., 1952).

For information about the magazines, see Frank Luther Mott, *A History of American Magazines*, Vols. IV–V (Cambridge, Mass., 1957, 1968), and Theodore Peterson, *Magazines in the Twentieth Century* (Urbana, 1964).

The classic study of the muckrakers is and will remain Louis Filler, *Crusaders for American Liberalism* (Yellow Springs, 1939). David Chalmers, *The Social and Political Ideas of the Muckrakers* (New York, 1964) and Harold S. Wilson, *McClure's Magazine and the Muckrakers* (Princeton, 1970) offer general overviews. James Harvey Young, *The Toadstool Millionaires* (Princeton, 1961), and John Braeman, Robert H. Bremner and Everett Walters, eds., *Change and Continuity in Twentieth-Century America* (New York, 1964) contain excellent studies of the drug and the meat inspection campaigns.

The history of the muckrakers and the conservation controversy is to be found in Alpheus T. Mason, *Bureaucracy Convicts Itself* (New York, 1941), Elmo R. Richardson, *The Politics of Conservation* (Berkeley, 1962), and James Pennick, Jr., *Progressive Politics and Conservation* (Chicago, 1968).

For biographies for the muckrakers, read Louis Filler's, *The Unknown Edwin Markham* (Yellow Springs, 1966) and Charles Larsen's *Biography*

154

of Ben Lindsey (Chicago, 1971). Both Robert C. Bannister, Jr. (New Haven, 1966) and John E. Semonche (Chapel Hill, 1969) have written on *Ray Stannard Baker*, and biographies of Lincoln Steffens are currently being prepared by Justin Kaplan, Herbert Shapiro, and Harry Stein.

Reissues of muckrake writings are Ray Stannard Baker, *Following the Color Line*, Dewey Grantham, ed. (New York, 1908, 1964); Will Irwin, *The American Newspaper*, Clifford F. Weigle and David G. Clark, eds. (Ames, 1969); David Graham Phillips, *The Treason of the Senate*, George E. Mowry and Judson A. Grenier, eds. (Chicago, 1964); Lincoln Steffens, *The Shame of the Cities*, Louis Joughlin, ed. (New York, 1904, 1957), and Ida Tarbell, *The History of the Standard Oil Company*, David Chalmers, ed. (New York, 1904, 1968). Upton Sinclair's *The Jungle* (New York, 1906) has probably never been out of print.

William E. Leuchtenburg has edited a reissue of Walter Lippmann's classic commentary on the progressive era, *Drift and Mastery* (New York, 1914, 1961), and Lincoln Steffens' son Peter has kept his father's delightful *The Autobiography of Lincoln Steffens* (New York, 1931, 1958) in print.

Collections of muckrake writing are *The Muckrakers*, edited by Arthur and Lila Weinberg (New York, 1961) and Harvey Swados, ed., *Years of Conscience* (Cleveland, 1962). *The Muckrakers and American Society*, Herbert Shapiro, ed. (Boston, 1968) contains a cross section of writings about them, and the historical role of muckraking is studied in *Muckraking, Past, Present and Future*, John Harrison and Harry Stein, eds. (University Park, Pa., 1973).

Index

SELECTED LIST OF ANVIL BOOKS